Darling Ros

Merry Christmas! 19

Wishing you amazing meals,
fun times + lots of laughter

love for 2019

Jane

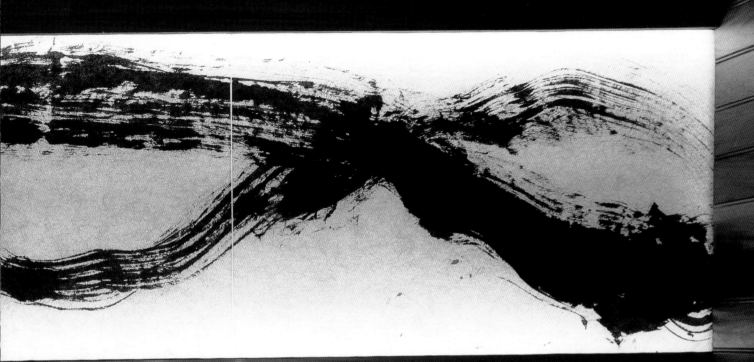

by NIC WATT

PHOTOGRAPHY BY BABICHE MARTENS

A&U

For Jas —
for all things
connected to the sea.

CONTENTS

FOREWORD

I first met Nic Watt over a delicious tuna and caviar tartare and some amazing lamb chops with a Korean sauce in 2004 when he opened and co-founded Roka restaurant on London's Charlotte Street. I'd been aware of Nic previously, from when he was working at Nobu in London before heading back to New Zealand to become executive chef at Huka Lodge. I'd followed his career when I could, admiring this fellow New Zealander's determination, enviable talent and hard work. He has had, and continues to have, a fantastic career in the kitchen, but he's also a smart businessman and operator.

In 2012 I was holding my second Dining for a Difference dinner at SKYCITY, a thirteen-chef dinner charity event raising money for Leukaemia and Blood Cancer New Zealand. Every dinner I get to choose and invite chefs from around New Zealand and Australia, along with one international name. On the night, chefs draw the names of the table hosts out of a hat. I'd felt SKYCITY should have a contemporary Japanese restaurant in their stable, and in my mind Nic was the perfect chef to do that, so I'd asked him to come and be part of this fabulous evening. Nic flew out to cook at the dinner, wooed the guests, and fortuitously got to cook for Nigel Morrison's table on the night. The rest, as they say, is history. Nigel and Nic hit it off and Nigel could see the talent in front of him. And several years later, with Nic and his family relocating from Wimbledon to Auckland, Masu is now firmly on New Zealand's culinary radar, having won Metro Supreme Restaurant of the Year and gaining two chefs hats in the Cuisine awards, amongst other things. Masu - it may be the name of the simple wooden box sake is served in, but it is so much more than that. And it's fantastic to have Nic part of the team here in Auckland.

Peter Gordon - chef, restaurateur and friend
London 2015

INTRODUCTION

THE NAME

A masu box is a square wooden box that was used to ration rice in Japan during the feudal period. Today masu boxes are smaller and used for drinking sake out of. If you came to my house I would put your cup into a masu box and pour till the sake overflowed into the box itself. This custom symbolises abundance, prosperity, goodwill and giving more than people expect; this is the essence of the Masu dining experience.

I would really like to take credit for the clever name, but I have to acknowledge Nigel Morrison as it was definitely a collaborative effort.

THE RESTAURANT

Masu has been two decades in the making. So many experiences and colourful characters from the last 23 years of my culinary career have contributed in some way to this restaurant. From my early days in Japan, when I could only count to 10 and say hello in Japanese, to meeting the gorgeous waitress in London who would become my wife, to being the global chief operating officer of Roka group – all of this is reflected somewhere in the bustling, dynamic space that is Masu. Masu is the realisation of a long-held dream to open my own restaurant in this city I hold so dear.

Masu is, of course, Japanese in every way: the Obi Room decorated with sashes from the national costume; the home-made shochu in jars at the bar; the chefs' incredible skill in slicing sashimi. But there are a lot of Kiwi touches too – I always smile when I see someone standing at the bar with an LwP (lemon and pineapple shochu, that is; we've even had a special retro bottle made). And, although the cuisine is Japanese, the salmon comes from Nelson, the wasabi root from Hokitika and the ginger stem from Pukekohe. At Masu, we love New Zealand produce.

The Kiwi sense of laid-back casual fun is also embedded in our ethos. While we've certainly had some big deals signed here during high-powered business lunches, this is first and foremost a place to relax, have fun and laugh loudly over good food. There are no rules about what you can eat at the bar or in the restaurant, for lunch or for dinner, and we regularly have groups who come for lunch and end up staying all day. My wife Kelly and I have achieved the balance we always wanted: high-end food prepared with a level of skill and passion found only in the world's top restaurants but without a trace of formality or austerity.

A lot of thought and detail has gone into every part of Masu. The robata grill can be seen from any seat in the house, the chopsticks are lined up with military precision and the ice for our shochu is hand-sawn from a huge deoxygenated block so it doesn't dilute your beverage. But we have made sure that all of this is designed to enhance your experience, not intimidate you.

We don't care what you order, or whether your wine or sake matches your food perfectly. We welcome your kids – in fact we provide origami kits for them so you can enjoy your meal – and we don't care if you're the hippest of hipsters or celebrating your seventy-fifth birthday in your twinset and pearls. We love for you to be entertained too, and encourage the swinging-round of chairs to check out the flames, culinary craftmanship and high-energy excitement of our very open kitchen.

Of course the quality of our cuisine is paramount, and we hire our staff very carefully to make sure of this. When I found out Masu was going to become a reality, I made one phone call to one chef in London, and thank goodness he said yes. Darren Johnson is one of the best in the business and is executive chef of our incredible kitchen. Everything is made from scratch, aggressive behaviour is not tolerated and we would most certainly not be the success we are without him at the helm.

It's the same with front of house. Truly personable and attentive waitstaff are crucial and we always employ people with that little spark. A restaurant with great food but no personality is not a fun place to be. We love our customers and, while it's wonderful to see new people discovering us, we also really enjoy seeing regular faces reappear at the bar, tables or grill. We're proud to be a favourite spot for many, and we hope customers always leave feeling as excited about the Japanese dining experience as we are.

MY BACKGROUND

I started cooking when I was 18 and by 21 was head chef of a busy Auckland restaurant. Like most young men, I thought I knew it all, so I packed my bags and knives and headed to Sydney. Turns out I didn't know as much as I thought, so I went on to learn some more.

It was common at that time for chefs to go to Europe, but the well-trod path has never really appealed and I decided Japan was for me. As an Antipodean, I love seafood and I saw no better place to master the preparation and cooking of it.

It was my time there that gave me a proper understanding, and undying passion for

Japan, its cuisine and its culture. I lived, worked and socialised with Japanese people and fell in love with their food, customs and outlook on life. Working at the Park Hyatt Tokyo taught me skills that are very much relevant to Masu today.

After 18 months I took this knowledge to London where I applied for a stage (a trial shift) at Aubergine, Gordon Ramsay's restaurant, and also applied at Nobu Matsuhisa's eponymous restaurant. I got a job offer from both Gordon and Nobu; I took up the Nobu offer. Nobu was groundbreaking at that time – one of the first Japanese restaurants without all the usual formalities that come with that type of cuisine. There people laughed and spoke loudly at tables with no cloths on them, rather than in hushed tones in a staid setting. We regularly served the likes of Madonna, Elton John, Grace Jones and Robert DeNiro.

One day at work a beautiful English waitress, Kelly, asked me where to find the chilli sauce, even though I was new. I was so focused on my tempura oysters I didn't realise she wasn't actually looking for the sauce at all! Seventeen years and two kids later, she's still by my side and has made the Masu dream a reality with her deep understanding of front-of-house operations.

Other great roles followed, including relaunching the Park Hyatt Rib Room and Oyster Bar in London, but we eventually left England, Chicago bound. Unfortunately the fateful events of 9/11 diverted us home temporarily but, serendipitously, I got a job offer from Huka Lodge. Changing course slightly, I accepted and we were there for three wonderful years. It was at Huka Lodge that I put out my first cookbook.

In 2004, an offer from a great friend and mentor, Rainer Becker, presented an opportunity in London I couldn't refuse – the chance to help him open a new restaurant specialising in high-end Japanese cuisine. Roka was a hit and in our first year we won Best Oriental Restaurant of the Year in the Tio Pepe London Restaurant Awards. My role, as chief operating officer, was to open branches in the United States, Hong Kong and at other locations in London. I relished this position, taking exceptional Japanese cuisine to new territories.

Fate stepped in again in 2011 when Peter Gordon asked me to cook for a fundraiser in Auckland. I ended up cooking Roka food for Nigel Morrison's table (the CEO of SKYCITY). I really enjoyed being back home and clearly remember the moment when, driving along the waterfront, I realised how gorgeous Auckland was. I thought, *You idiot! What are you doing over there when all of this is right here?*

Fifteen months later we were back in Aotearoa with the intention of finally opening our own place. Nigel still remembered that meal and soon convinced us to join the SKYCITY family. We are so grateful to him for his enthusiasm, for engaging with us on such a personal level, and for supporting us in this venture. I've opened a few restaurants now, but the first night at Masu was by far the most nerve-wracking. It's one thing to open a restaurant overseas, but bringing everything back home is something else.

I needn't have been so worried. Masu has been successful beyond all our hopes and won a Metro Restaurant of the Year Supreme Winner Award, as well as the Cuisine Best New Restaurant Award in its first year. With the support of great staff and of Nigel and his team, Kelly and I couldn't be happier to be running this fun, high-energy restaurant in one of the best cities in the world.

THE COOKBOOK

I have written this cookbook to share my passion for Japanese food with home cooks. There is a common misconception that it's a complicated cuisine requiring a lot of time and effort, but this is not necessarily true. It's more about understanding the ingredients and their uses, as most of us in New Zealand haven't grown up with them in our family pantry.

While there are Japanese dishes that look like works of art and take hours to construct, there are also many simple everyday dishes that are easy to prepare once you know how. And ingredients are getting easier to source by the day; no longer only the domain of speciality stores, you'll find many ingredients in general Asian shops or even at your local supermarket.

Japanese food is enormously versatile, too. From feeding a crowd of hungry 10-year-olds after football, to family barbecues, to trying to impress that all-important first date, there's something easy for all occasions.

So read the section on key ingredients, stock up your pantry and dive in. I guarantee you'll be surprised at how easy it is to turn out something pretty impressive. I don't want this book to sit on your bookshelf or your coffee table, I want it to be in your kitchen – and even end up with some soy sauce stains on the pages.

Nic Watt
July, 2015

JAPANESE
PANTRY, TOOLS
& ETIQUETTE

JAPANESE
PANTRY

1 ___ MOMIJI OROSHI
chilli daikon paste

2 ___ BENI SHOGA
red pickled ginger

3 ___ KATSUOBUSHI
dried bonito flakes used for making dashi

4 ___ MIRIN
sweet cooking rice wine

5 ___ WASABI
dried powdered wasabi

6 ___ LA-YU
spiced oil used for seasoning

7 ___ SHOYU
soy sauce made from fermented soy beans

8 ___ SANSHO
prickly ash tree pepper spice

9 ___ SHIITAKE
dried aromatic mushroom

10 ___ SAIKYO MISO
sweet white miso

11 ___ SHICHIMI
seven-spice powder

12 ___ ATARI GOMA
sesame paste

13 ___ GOCHUJANG
Korean hot pepper paste

14 ___ YONEZU
rice vinegar

15 ___ SAKE
rice wine

16 ___ MUGI MISO
miso paste made from fermented barley

17 ___ ICHIMI
single chilli powder

18 ___ YUZOKOSHŌ
a paste made from chilli pepper, Yuzu peel and salt

19 ___ KOMBU
dried seaweed, used for stocks

JAPANESE
TOOLS

1,2,3 __ YANA GIBA
Japanese hand-made sashimi knives

4 __ DEBA
fish filleting knife

5 __ IPPON PICK
single-prong ice pick used for chipping ice

6 __ SANPON PICK
tri-prong ice pick used for holding ice

7 __ KOHAKE
very small pastry brush used for seasoning nigiri

8 __ MORIBASHI
cooking and kitchen chopsticks

9 __ HAKE
pastry brush

10 __ SURIKOGI BOU
muddling stick

11 __ MASU
masu box

12 __ TAKE ZUTSU
bamboo sake cup

13 __ MAKISU
bamboo mat used for maki sushi

14 __ KOSHAMOJI
wooden spoon

15 __ HERA
wooden paddle

16 __ KUSHI
wooden skewers

17 __ HOUCHOU MIGAKI
knife-polishing and cleaning stone

18 __ SAMEGAWA OROSHI
sharkskin-covered wasabi paddle

19 __ TAKE BASAMI
bamboo sugar tweezers

20 __ HISHAKU
bamboo ladle

21 __ KIBAKO
cedar-wood serving tray

25

JAPANESE EATING
ETIQUETTE

As with all cuisines, there are some things considered polite at the Japanese dinner table and some not. Here's a quick guide to the basic dos and don'ts.

BEFORE EATING

It is customary to say 'Itadakimasu' (literally 'I shall receive') before eating a meal, and 'Gochiso-sama deshita' (literally 'That was a feast') to the host afterwards or to the restaurant staff as you leave.

Before eating, most dining places will provide either a hot towel or a plastic-wrapped wet napkin. This is for cleaning your hands prior to eating, rather than after. It is considered rude to use this to wash your face or any part of the body other than the hands.

DRINKING

Even in informal situations, drinking alcohol starts with a toast - 'Kanpai' - when everyone is ready. It is not customary to pour yourself a drink; rather, people are expected to keep each other's drinks topped up.

EATING

Rice or soup is eaten by picking the bowl up with the left hand and using chopsticks with the right. Bowls of soup, noodle soup, donburi or ochazuke may be lifted to the mouth, but not white rice. Noodles are slurped.

Soy sauce is not generally poured over food at the table; there is usually a dipping dish. In particular, soy sauce should never be poured onto rice or soup.

Blowing one's nose at the table is considered extremely offensive.

It is customary to eat rice to the last grain. Being a fussy eater is frowned upon, and it's not common to make special requests or ask for substitutions at restaurants. It is considered ungrateful to make these requests, especially in circumstances where you are being hosted, such as a business dinner. Good manners show that you respect the selections of your host.

CHOPSTICK ETIQUETTE

When you are not using your chopsticks and when you have finished eating, lay them down in front of you with the tip to the left.

Never leave chopsticks sticking vertically out of your rice, as this is how they are ritually offered to the dead at the altar or shrine at a funeral.

Hold your chopsticks towards the top end, not in the middle or bottom, narrow third.

Do not point at anything or anyone with your chopsticks. Don't move your chopsticks around in the air too much or play with them.

Do not move plates or bowls around with your chopsticks. When taking food from a communal dish - unless you are with family or very close friends - turn the chopsticks around to grab the food; this is considered cleaner. Don't spear food with your chopsticks.

If sharing food with someone else, move it directly from one plate to another. Passing food from one pair of chopsticks to another is a funeral rite (the bones of the cremated body are passed from person to person that way).

MENUS

SUMMER
FAST AND
FUN

—

GATHERINGS AND DINNER PARTIES

—

DATE NIGHT
TO IMPRESS

—

SOFT-SHELL CRAB AND
KIMCHI FUTO MAKI ROLL
page 63

SPICY MISO CRAYFISH TACOS
WITH TOASTED SESAME SLAW
page 106

GRILLED ASPARAGUS,
PAN-FRIED QUAIL EGG AND SOY
page 143

WAGYU BEEF SIRLOIN,
BONE MARROW AND SHIITAKE
page 164

MASU CEDAR ROAST CHOCOLATE
AND GREEN TEA PUDDING
page 182

SEARED,
CURED
AND RAW

SEARED TUNA TATAKI AND GRAPEFRUIT ESCABECHE

COOK TIME
— **30 minutes**

SERVES
— **2**

This dish is all in the preparation. The escabeche will last in the fridge for future lunches or dinners, and is a great accompaniment to have handy. Then all you need on the day is a fresh piece of tuna and you are good to go.

GRAPEFRUIT ESCABECHE
— 100 ml (3½ fl oz) ponzu vinegar
— 125 ml (4 fl oz) soy sauce
— 2 tablespoons (1 fl oz) mirin
— 2 teaspoons sake
— 2 tablespoons sliced ginger
— 1 ruby grapefruit, sliced (skin on)
— 1 green chilli, sliced
— 100 ml (3½ fl oz) olive oil

— 1 x 200 g (7 oz) tuna loin
— olive oil
— sea salt and freshly cracked black pepper
— ½ cup daikon, finely sliced
— 1 teaspoon pickled wasabi
— garlic chips (see page 208)

Begin by combining the ponzu, soy sauce, mirin, sake and ginger in a medium-sized saucepan. Bring to a simmer over a medium heat to infuse, then remove from the heat and add the grapefruit and chilli. Allow to cool. Add the olive oil and store until needed. It will keep for a week in the fridge.

Lightly coat the tuna in olive oil and season liberally with salt and pepper. Heat a non-stick frying pan to smoking. Tataki means 'to sear' so that's what you do: sear the tuna for 30 seconds on each side. It should remain raw in the centre and be only just seared and crusted on the outside.

To serve, cut the tuna into bite-size slices and roll up sliced daikon, lay tuna over daikon and top with wasabi pickle, garlic chips and finish with a good splash of escabeche.

BEEF TATAKI,
GINGER PONZU,
GARLIC CHIPS

COOK TIME
— 30 minutes

SERVES
— 2

Beef tataki is a staple at many restaurants and has been on Masu's menu since the beginning. This is a great way to get a simple salad up and at the table.

— 1 x 200 g (7 oz) beef sirloin
— olive oil for cooking
— sea salt and freshly cracked black pepper

GINGER PONZU
— 1 tablespoon grated ginger
— 80 ml (2½ fl oz) ponzu vinegar
— 40 ml (1¼ fl oz) mirin
— 40 ml (1¼ fl oz) olive oil

TO SERVE
— 1 cup finely sliced daikon
— 1 tablespoon pickled wasabi
— 1 tablespoon garlic chips (see page 208)
— 1 pinch sliced chives

Lightly coat the beef in olive oil and season liberally with salt and pepper. Heat a sauté pan to smoking. Place the oiled and seasoned beef in the pan and sear on all four sides for about 30 seconds each side. Remove from the pan, allow to cool, then refrigerate so the beef firms up for slicing.

To make the ginger ponzu, simply place all of the ingredients in a mixing bowl and whisk lightly to combine. You are not trying to emulsify the dressing, so the oil should sit on top.

To serve, slice the beef into even bite-size slices. Twist the daikon into seven even bite-size balls. Lay the beef over the daikon, and spoon over the ginger ponzu. Finish with pickled wasabi, a garlic chip and a sliced chive.

TARTARE
OF SALMON, AVOCADO AND CAVIAR

PREP TIME
— 20 minutes

SERVES
— 2 sharing

This is my take on a classic tartare, only we serve it with salmon not beef. With any good tartare you need a means to carry it on the palate. You can serve this tartare with some plain wheat or rice crackers. At Masu we serve it with homemade sushi rice crackers.

— 1 x 100 g (3½ oz) salmon fillet, skinned and boned
— 1 tablespoon finely diced shallot
— 1 tablespoon ponzu vinegar
— 1 tablespoon olive oil
— ½ teaspoon ichimi chilli
— 1 egg yolk
— ¼ avocado
— juice of 1 lemon
— 2 tablespoons salmon caviar

Use a sharp knife to mince the salmon fillet down to a fine paste. In a medium-sized bowl mix the salmon, shallot, ponzu vinegar, olive oil, ichimi chilli and egg yolk with a fork to evenly incorporate all the ingredients.

Carefully spread the salmon mixture across two-thirds of a serving dish. Slice the avocado and squeeze over the lemon juice to prevent the avocado from going brown. Place this beside the salmon on your dish. Fill the remaining section of your tray with salmon caviar.

Serve with crackers and a spoon.

HOW TO PREPARE
SASHIMI

I have eaten a lot of so-called sashimi off the bait board on the back of a boat. While it might be raw, it is not sashimi.

In just a few simple steps, however, you can prepare some very fresh raw fish that you can call sashimi.

First you must iki the fish, piercing it just behind the eyes with an Ikigun. This is to stop any unwanted blood flow or further deterioration of the flesh when the fish is out of the water.

Don't leave your fish in a bucket in the sun. Place it straight into the fridge or a chilly bin to rest and cool. It is really important that the fish is laid flat so the meat and muscle can relax back into a natural position. You will need to rest the fish for at least 2 hours.

With a clean board and a sharp knife, fillet the fish in one section per fillet. Don't cut out the pin bones, as they are in some of the finest meat on the fillet; use tweezers or fine-nosed pliers to pull out the pin bones. Divide the fillet into the top section and the belly section. I almost always use the top section for cooking and the delicious, fatty belly section for sashimi.

Carefully remove the skin from the belly section and discard. Place the belly lengthways on your board and slice the fillet across the belly into slices about 3 mm thick. Ensure that you slice in a diagonal across the grain of the meat. This will give you textured but not chewy sashimi slices.

Serve the freshly cut belly slices with some wasabi and soy sauce.

TUNA THREE WAYS

This not so much a recipe as an explanation of how tuna is sectioned and why.

Tuna has three main cuts and sections. It is important to know and understand where in the fish these come from, how they vary in flavour and texture, and ultimately how this affects the price.

I often find the easiest way to define this is to say tuna store fat like men - that is, around the belly and love handles, leaving the legs lean.

OTORO

The belly is the fattiest, most highly prized section of the fish. It is light pink and heavily marbled with fat that melts in your mouth. A single slice of otoro served with fresh wasabi and soy sauce is one of the most renowned Japanese dishes in the world, yet also one of the simplest - just three pure ingredients. We can pay up $155 per kilogram for this section of the fish.

CHUTORO

The upper part of the tuna - or love handles! - is semi-fatty. This acts as insulation around the top section of the fish. The meat is lightly marbled and has a clean and full flavour. Tuna carry more chutoro than otoro, so the price is a little less and it is generally more readily available. I prefer to use chutoro for tataki and seared tuna dishes, as it has enough mineral flavour and a great balance of fat to carry through the dish.

AKAMI

The tail and rich red meat that surrounds the spine have a dark red colour with very low fat. You will find this cut to have a strong, clean mineral flavour and the largest percentage of meat. We use this for our maki rolls.

All of these cuts can be eaten as sashimi.

I was recently on a charter fishing trip for my best friend's stag do, and among the group were three chefs. We caught a beautiful skipjack tuna. This is a very small, bullet-like tuna with a high akami content. To the rest of the boat, this was bait for the bigger fish we were hoping to catch. But to the three chefs, Michael, Eugene and me, this was lunch - and as fresh as we could possibly get. We had our lunch; they said we ate bait! We are still divided on this.

— 1 block otoro (belly tuna)
— 1 block chutoro (semi-fatty tuna)
— 1 block akami (tail meat)

OTORO

CHUTORO

AKAMI

SALMON, SNAPPER, TREVALLY AND SCAMPI **SASHIMI**

PREP TIME
— 30 minutes

SERVES
— 2

On my final working day in Japan, my chefs took me out for a last supper, so to speak. They said I could order anything so, since I was a young chef spending most of my money on travel and exploring, I took this opportunity to order the live snapper from the tank. The sashimi chef filleted the fish right in front of me and served the sliced meat back onto the fish itself. The snapper was as fresh as; it had only moments ago been pulled out of the water. I had to cover up its eyes so it could not see me eating its own sashimi. The Japanese thought this was hilarious but accepted my pity for the fish – after all, I was a gaijin (foreigner).

— 1 salmon fillet, skinned and boned
— 1 snapper fillet, skinned and boned
— 1 trevally fillet, skinned and boned
— 1 scampi
— 1 tablespoon wasabi paste to serve
— 4 tablespoons soy sauce to serve

When serving sashimi it is always nice to be able to offer a few varieties of fish, for their different textures and colours. At Masu we cut all our soft-texture sashimi as atsuzukuri (thick-cut style) – the fisherman's way.

I have selected salmon as it is generally a restaurant favourite, snapper because it is a white fish that is commonly caught off the New Zealand shores, trevally for its great unique flavour and texture, and finally scampi as a crustacean that is seriously delicious and locally caught.

The important part here is knowing how to prepare and slice each different fish.

SALMON
I like to take the top shoulder section and trim it down so you have a slab three fingers wide and two fingers tall. Use a very sharp knife and, in a single action for each slice, cut three even pieces about 4 mm thick. Carefully, with as little handling and bruising as possible, present a fan of these on your plate.

SNAPPER
Slice the fillet in half lengthways, following the backbone line. I like to use the top section for sashimi. Angle your knife so you are cutting across the grain of the meat and slice three thin 2 mm slices. At the base of each slice, rotate the knife to give a slightly thicker edge. This edge will help catch the soy sauce when you dunk the fish. Pinch and slightly roll each piece to give some shape and texture when presenting it on the plate.

CONTINUED OVERLEAF . . .

TREVALLY

I use a mid-section of the fillet. With trevally you will have a small bloodline that – contrary to popular belief – gives a nice rich flavour. Turn the fillet so the bloodline is at the top and slice three even pieces about 4 mm thick. Carefully plate and fan out, highlighting the bloodline.

SCAMPI

First remove the head from the tail. Keep the head as a garnish and, for the brave ones, something to eat. Cut up the back of the shell with scissors and lift the meat out. Remove the vein from the tail. Cut three even bite-size pieces across the tail and lay them back into the tail shell, or laid on the plate next to it. Place on your serving plate with the head.

Serve the freshly sliced sashimi with wasabi and soy sauce.

LET'S GET
ROLLING

CUCUMBER AND PICKLED PLUM
HOSO MAKI ROLL

PREP TIME
— **15 minutes**

MAKES
— **1 maki roll**

Hoso maki is believed to be the original form of rolled sushi, as it uses a single or minimal filling. With a maki roll it's always about the freshness, so make them as close to serving as possible. The basic fundamentals of maki are room temperature rice and crisp dry nori. Once you have mastered the small thin roll, it will put you in good stead to move on to bigger and inside-out rolls. This elegant bite-size sushi makes for great finger food. I often use hoso maki on tasting menus as it works as great palate cleanser and I love its simplicity.

— 1 toasted nori sheet
— ½ cup cooked sushi rice (see page 206)
— 1 cucumber baton, 1 cm square x 18 cm long (½ in x 7 in)
— 3 pickled plums, stones removed
— 1 teaspoon toasted sesame seeds
— wasabi to serve
— pickled ginger to serve
— soy sauce to serve

Begin by folding your nori sheet in half so it breaks neatly in two. You should have two equal 10 cm x 20 cm (4 in x 8 in) rectangles.

Lay a half sheet of nori on a bamboo mat in a horizontal position. Take your rice and spread it from the bottom long edge to about 1 cm (½ in) from the top edge. Place your cucumber in the centre of the rice, line the pickled plums against the cucumber edge and sprinkle the sesame seeds all over the rice.

Using your bamboo mat, lift the bottom edge of the nori and rice and, like a wave dumping, roll over and curl under to form your maki roll.

Run a damp finger across the unfilled edge of the nori to ensure it sticks. Roll up completely and give it a final gentle squeeze to form.

Slice into six even pieces and serve with wasabi, pickled ginger and soy.

SPICY TUNA
URA MAKI ROLL

PREP TIME
— 15 minutes

MAKES
— 1 maki roll

*Spicy tuna is a
benchmark of many
Japanese restaurants,
and will generally be one
of the most popular rolls.
This inside-out roll looks
harder to make than it
actually is. The key here is
to line your bamboo mat
with cling film to prevent
the rice from sticking to
it. This style of roll is the
basis for other modern
versions of sushi like the
California roll.*

— 1 toasted nori sheet
— ½ cup cooked sushi rice
  (see page 206)
— 2½ tablespoons finely
  diced raw tuna
— 2 fingers avocado
— 1 tablespoon finely sliced
  spring onion
— 1 tablespoon basic
  mayonnaise
— 1 teaspoon finely diced
  jalapeño pepper
— 1 tablespoon shichimi
  pepper
— 1 raw tuna slice, 2 cm x
  20 cm x ½ cm thick (¾ in x
  8 in x ¼ in)
— 1 teaspoon soy sauce plus
  extra to serve
— wasabi to serve
— pickled ginger to serve

Begin by folding your nori sheet in half so it breaks neatly
in two. You should have two equal 10 cm x 20 cm (4 in x 8
in) rectangles.

Line your bamboo mat with cling film and lay the nori
on the mat in a horizontal position. Take your rice and
spread it from the bottom long edge to about 1 cm (½ in)
from the top edge. Now flip the rice and nori over so the
rice is facing the cling film.

Place your diced tuna in the centre of the nori, and add
the avocado and spring onion on top.

Mix the mayo with the jalapeño pepper and spread in a
line on top of the diced tuna.

Using your bamboo mat, lift the bottom edge of the nori
and rice and, like a wave dumping, roll over and curl
under to form your maki roll.

Run a damp finger across the unfilled edge of the nori
to ensure it sticks. Roll up completely and give it a final
gentle squeeze to form.

You should have your rice on the outside with your
nori on the inside. Dust the outside of the roll with the
shichimi pepper.

Lay your raw tuna slice over the top of the roll and
brush the top of the tuna with soy sauce.

Slice into six even pieces and serve with soy sauce,
wasabi and pickled ginger.

SOFT-SHELL CRAB AND KIMCHI
FUTO MAKI ROLL

PREP TIME
— 15 minutes

MAKES
— 1 maki roll

Futo maki has four or more fillings, making a bigger, fuller roll. The sheet of daikon on the exterior gives this roll a great contrast, visually and texturally. These rolls are often called date maki, or dandy rolls, because of their colourful and beautiful fillings. The rolling technique is the same as the thinner hoso maki but needs a little more skill and care to ensure all your fillings stay neatly inside. You will sometimes see futo maki in kaleidoscope patterns – for the very adventurous . . .

- 200 ml (7 fl oz) rice bran oil for frying
- 1 toasted nori sheet
- ½ cup cooked sushi rice (see page 206)
- 1 soft-shell crab
- 1 tablespoon potato starch
- 2 tablespoons sliced kimchi (see page 74)
- 3 cucumber batons, ½ cm square x 12 cm long (¼ in square x 4½ in)
- 3 chives
- 1 daikon sheet, 10 cm x 15 cm (4 in x 6 in)
- soy sauce to serve
- wasabi to serve
- Nic's pickled cucumber chilli to serve (see page 76)

Begin by folding your nori sheet in half so it breaks neatly in two. You should have two equal 10 cm x 20 cm (4 in x 8 in) rectangles.

Lay one half of the nori sheet on the bamboo mat in a vertical position. Take your rice and spread it from the bottom short edge, leaving about 4 cm clear at the top edge.

Heat your rice bran oil to about 180°C (350°F).

Pat dry your soft-shell crab and dust with the potato starch. Fry the crab in the rice bran oil until crisp, about 3 minutes, then drain on absorbent paper and cut it in half, ready to roll.

Place the crisp crab in the centre of the rice, and add the kimchi, cucumber and chives to the side.

Using your bamboo mat, lift the bottom edge of the nori and rice and, like a wave dumping, roll over and curl under to form your maki roll.

Run a damp finger across the unfilled edge of the nori to ensure it sticks. Roll up completely and give it a final gentle squeeze to form.

Finally, lay your daikon sheet on the bench and roll the finished maki in the daikon sheet.

Slice into six even pieces and serve with soy sauce, wasabi and pickled cucumber chilli.

WAGYU BEEF GUNKAN MAKI AND MISO-CURED QUAIL YOLK

— 15 minutes + 12 hours
   curing time

MAKES
— 6 gunkan maki

This dish dates back to my days in London at Roka, where we served a very similar dish with caviar. However, I prefer the creamy fullness the egg yolk gives the beef. I use this dish as an icebreaker – getting food onto people's palates quickly is the key to any great event. Gunkan means 'battleship', hence the shape, and is a form of nigiri sushi.

MISO-CURED QUAIL YOLKS
— 3 tablespoons sweet white
   miso paste
— 3 tablespoons sake
— 6 quail eggs

— 1 toasted nori sheet
— 60 g (3½ oz) Wagyu beef,
   finely diced
— 1 teaspoon ponzu vinegar
— 1 teaspoon soy sauce
— ½ teaspoon ginger paste
— freshly cracked black
   pepper
— ½ cup cooked sushi rice
   (see page 206)
— 1 tablespoon finely sliced
   spring onion

Start with the quail yolks. Mix the white miso and sake together in a small bowl. Crack and separate the eggs, carefully dropping the yolks into the miso mixture. Cure in the fridge for about 12 hours.

Cut your toasted nori sheet into six even strips, 3 cm x 15 cm (1¼ in x 6 in).

In a small bowl, mix together the Wagyu beef, ponzu vinegar, soy sauce, ginger paste and pepper. This is like a tartare base.

Form six thumb-sized logs of rice and wrap the rice in the nori. Stand each gunkan on its end, and top with the seasoned Wagyu beef. Carefully spoon out a cured quail's yolk and place on top. Garnish with finely sliced spring onion.

WILD PRAWN
BO ZUSHI

PREP TIME
— 15 minutes + 5 hours
   marinating time

MAKES
— 6 bo zushi

This is a very simple and delicious log-style sushi. Traditionally it is made using a square box to press the marinated fish onto the sushi rice and then it is cut into neat rectangles. At Masu we follow this approach but press the rice into the natural shape of the prawn tail.

PRAWNS
— 6 XL wild-caught tiger prawns
— 75 ml (2¼ fl oz) ponzu vinegar
— 4 drops chilli oil
— 1 teaspoon dried smoked chilli
— ½ cup fresh coriander leaves and stems

— 1 ripe avocado
— juice of 2 lemons
— sea salt and freshly cracked black pepper
— 1 cup cooked sushi rice (see page 206)
— 1 long mild red chilli, sliced to serve
— 1 pinch edible flowers to serve

Begin by removing and discarding the heads of the prawns. Carefully remove the tail shell to the last part of the tail section – you want to keep the last segment. With a small knife, butterfly the prawn by cutting from the base to the top, but don't cut right through. Remove the vein and press the prawn out flat, into a nice even butterfly.

To make the marinade, combine the ponzu vinegar, chilli oil and smoked chilli. Use your hands to squash and bruise the coriander, breaking out the aroma and flavour. Add to the marinade. Spoon together in a small bowl.

Place the butterflied prawns in the marinade and leave in the fridge for 5 hours until ready to serve.

Place the avocado flesh and lemon juice in a food processor and purée to a smooth paste. Season with salt and pepper.

Form the rice into even finger-size logs. You don't have to be too precise as the next step is to lay a prawn tail on the rice logs and bring the sides of the prawn tail over the rice. You want the prawn to go back to its natural shape. Use a pastry brush to brush the marinade over the prawn, giving it shine and finished colour.

Serve with small dollops of the avocado purée and sprinkle over the sliced red chilli and edible flowers.

SALMON AVOCADO
TEMAKI CONE

PREP TIME
— 15 minutes

MAKES
— 1 temaki cone

Temaki can be made with almost any filling. I like them because they are made in the hand and designed to be eaten with your hands – a great snack that is fast to prepare and super-tasty.

— 1 toasted nori sheet
— ½ cup cooked sushi rice (see page 206)
— 1 fresh shiso leaf
— 2 raw salmon pieces (about 55 g), sliced
— 1 finger avocado
— 1 tablespoon salmon roe
— 1 teaspoon toasted sesame seeds
— soy sauce to serve
— wasabi to serve
— pickled ginger to serve

Begin by folding your nori sheet in half so it breaks neatly in two. You should have two equal 10 cm x 20 cm (4 in x 8 in) rectangles.

You make temaki in your hands. Hold one half of the nori sheet and spread the rice onto half of the sheet, so you have a square of rice and a square of toasted nori. Place the shiso leaf on the rice, then add the salmon and avocado. Take the bottom corner of nori with the rice on it and lift it on a diagonal to the opposite edge of the rice to form a cone. Then continue rolling and the whole piece will form neatly into a cone shape.

Top the temaki with salmon roe and toasted sesame seeds.

Serve with soy sauce, wasabi and pickled ginger.

SALADS AND
SHARING

HOME-MADE
KIMCHI CHILLI
CABBAGE

PREP TIME
— 2 days

MAKES
— 1 jar

*This is a super-simple way
to prepare cabbage: it's
hot, it's juicy and it will get
everyone's tastebuds talking.*

— 2 Chinese cabbages
— 2 tablespoons sea salt
— 190 ml (6½ fl oz) kimchi no
  moto sauce
— 1 teaspoon caster sugar
— ½ teaspoon Korean dried
  chilli powder
— zest of ½ ruby grapefruit
— 4 spring onions

Cut out the core of the cabbages and remove any damaged
leaves. Soak the cabbages in salted water overnight until
the leaves become tender. Drain off the water.

Combine the kimchi no moto sauce, caster sugar, dried
chilli powder and grapefruit zest.

In a large jar, layer the cabbage with the whole spring
onions through it. Cover and coat with the kimchi no moto
sauce mixture. Allow to stand for 24 hours before serving.

This kimchi will keep for six weeks.

Kimchi

1·4·15

NIC'S CUCUMBER CHILLI **PICKLE**

PREP TIME
— 15 minutes

MAKES
— 1 small bowl

This super-quick and super-tasty little number goes with almost any grilled food. It's a great recipe to have up your sleeve and only takes 15 minutes.

— 1 telegraph cucumber
— 2 pinches sea salt
— 1 long red chilli
— 100 ml (3½ fl oz) sushi vinegar (see page 206)

Halve the cucumber and use a spoon to scrape out the seeds. Slice the cucumber into bite-size chunks.

Sprinkle with sea salt and allow to stand for 10 minutes. The water will be drawn out of the cucumber and it will soften.

While the cucumber is softening, blacken the whole chilli over an open flame. Finely chop it all, seeds and blackened skin, to a coarse paste.

Wash the salt off the cucumber, pour over the vinegar and add the blackened chilli paste. Mix and serve.

WHITEBAIT SUSHI OMELETTE

COOK TIME
— 30 minutes

SERVES
— 4

I think everyone in New Zealand has a love of whitebait. This recipe is a great way to bring the delicious flavours together with egg. It can be made a little in advance, so is nice to have prepared before guests arrive.

— 125 ml (4 fl oz) dashi (see page 209)
— 1½ tablespoons sake
— 1½ tablespoons mirin
— 12 eggs
— vegetable oil for frying
— 1 cup whitebait
— rice or mayonnaise to serve

In a small saucepan, combine the dashi, sake and mirin, and bring to the boil. Boil for 1 minute to evaporate the alcohol, then allow to cool.

Beat the eggs in a large bowl and slowly add the cooled dashi mixture to incorporate. Strain.

Gently heat a square Japanese omelette pan, then lightly grease with the vegetable oil. Pour in about a sixth of the egg mixture and tilt the pan so the egg spreads in a thin, flat layer. Cook until the egg begins to set, then sprinkle a sixth of the whitebait over the top. Now tilt the pan and, using chopsticks or a spatula, fold the omelette into thirds back across the pan to form a neat folded roll.

Keep the first omelette in the pan and repeat with another sixth of egg mixture. Lift the cooked omelette so the new mixture spreads under it. Cook and add the whitebait as before. Now start rolling from the top of the pan, where the first roll is sitting, back towards the handle. Push the new larger roll to the back of the pan. Repeat four more times, adding a new layer to the roll each time.

Once you've finished cooking all the layers, keeping the shape, remove the omelette from the pan and wrap it in a sushi mat. Allow to cool to room temperature.

Serve sliced over rice as nigiri or warm with mayonnaise.

SPIDER
SLIDER

COOK TIME
— 15 minutes

MAKES
— 3 sliders

This slider is one of many brilliant creative moments from Darren, Masu's executive chef, and it's a star in the kitchen. It's not actually on the menu but if you ask for a spider slider you will get a knowing nod in return. We sell hundreds of these, you have just to be in the know . . . so I guess now you are!

The squid-ink brioche is not a must – you can use plain sliders – but it adds a great visual and the squid ink imparts the flavour of the sea.

— 200 ml (7 fl oz) rice bran oil
— 3 tablespoons basic mayonnaise (see page 205)
— 1 teaspoon yuzu koshu paste
— 1½ soft-shell crabs
— 2 tablespoons potato starch
— 3 squid-ink brioche slider buns
— ½ cup baby spinach leaves

Heat the rice bran oil to about 180°C (350°F).

Combine the mayonnaise with the yuzu koshu paste.

Pat dry the soft-shell crabs and dust with the potato starch.

Fry the crabs in the hot oil until crispy, about 3 minutes. Drain and cut in half.

Halve the slider buns and toast the insides.

To build the sliders, add a spoon of mayo to each brioche base followed with a few spinach leaves, a crispy crab half, and close with a bun top. Serve hot.

OCTOPUS
CARPACCIO

COOK TIME

— 40 minutes + 40 minutes
chilling time

SERVES

— 3

*Octopus is one of my
favourite dishes. It's not to
everyone's taste, but those
who do enjoy it love this
carpaccio version for its
clean, bright flavours.*

— 1 southern octopus
— 1 cup chopped daikon
— 4 celery stalks
— sea salt

DRESSING
— 1 tablespoon olive oil
— 1 teaspoon lemon juice
— 1 teaspoon soy sauce
— 3 drops chilli oil

TO SERVE
— 1 fennel bulb, very finely
sliced lengthways
— 200 ml (7 fl oz) iced water
— juice of 1 lemon
— 1 teaspoon dried chilli
flakes
— 1 sliced red radish

Ask your fish supplier for tenderised octopus to save you
the job of beating it tender yourself. Place a muslin cloth
on top of a sushi mat, ready to roll up.

Cut the tentacles off the octopus, and place five end-to-
end on the muslin to ensure an even-sized roll. Roll up
firmly, using butcher's twine to tie the mat up tightly.
Then wrap in tin foil.

Place the daikon, celery and salt in a saucepan of water
and bring to the boil. Add the octopus and simmer for
30 minutes. Drain immediately and place in the freezer
for 40 minutes, then transfer to the fridge before the
octopus freezes.

Make the dressing by combining all the ingredients.

Place the fennel in the iced water and lemon juice so the
fennel curls up.

Slice the octopus thinly and place on the drained fennel.
Serve with a good splash of the dressing and finish with a
good sprinkle of the dried chilli and sliced red radish.

PORK AND KIMCHI **GYOZA**

COOK TIME
— 30 minutes

MAKES
— 6 gyoza

Hot and tasty gyoza are a staple in almost all Japanese izakaya – the perfect snack with beer or sake. There are so many variations of gyoza; try swapping the pork for prawns in this recipe.

GYOZA
— 200 g (7 oz) pork mince
— 200 g (7 oz) kimchi, shredded (see page 74)
— 1 tablespoon soy sauce
— 1 tablespoon mirin
— 1 green chilli, finely chopped
— 6 gyoza wrappers

TO SERVE
— ¼ cucumber
— 60 ml (2 fl oz) sushi vinegar (see page 206)
— rice bran oil for cooking
— 1 teaspoon toasted sesame seeds

Simply combine the pork mince, kimchi, soy sauce, mirin and chilli for the filling.

Add a tablespoon of filling to each gyoza wrapper. Dab your finger in water and run it around the edge of the wrapper, then fold it in half and pinch the edges to form your gyoza. Repeat with the remaining filling and wrappers.

Halve the cucumber and scrape the seeds out with a spoon. Slice thinly and marinate in the sushi vinegar for 10 minutes.

Heat a frying pan to medium with a touch of rice bran oil. Pan-fry the gyoza until lightly coloured on the base, then add ½ cup (4 fl oz) of water and cover with a lid to steam through. The wrappers should have cooked clear and the water steamed out.

Serve with the pickled cucumber and toasted sesame seeds.

GRAPEFRUIT-CURED RED GURNARD AND BUCKWHEAT RICE

— 1 ruby grapefruit, skin on,
  sliced (reserve 2 segments
  for serving)
— zest of ½ an orange
— 1 cup bonito flakes
— 1 red chilli, sliced
— 2 tablespoons sliced ginger
— 125 ml (4 fl oz) mirin
— 375 ml (13 fl oz) ponzu
  vinegar
— 375 ml (13 fl oz) soy sauce
— 80 ml (2½ fl oz) yuzu juice
— 2 x 120 g red gurnard fillets,
  skin on, scaled and boned
— 1 carrot, cut into fine
  julienne
— 1 celery stalk, cut into fine
  julienne
— ½ sweet potato, cut into
  fine julienne

BUCKWHEAT RICE
— 1 cup cooked sushi rice
  (see page 206)
— 1 tablespoon buckwheat
— 1 tablespoon genmai cha
  tea leaves
— 1 toasted nori sheet

COOK TIME
— 30 minutes + 2 hours
  curing time

SERVES
— 2

*Gurnard is one of my all-time
favourite fish. It is totally
under-rated. Yes, it's bony,
but once you have removed
the bones the white flesh is
sweet and fine. I served this
beautiful fish to Her Majesty
the Queen back in 2002.*

To make the marinade, combine the ruby grapefruit, orange zest, bonito flakes, red chilli, ginger, mirin, ponzu vinegar, soy sauce and yuzu juice in a medium-sized saucepan and heat but don't boil. Remove from the heat and allow to cool.

Once the marinade is cool, divide it into one-third and two-thirds portions. Place the gurnard fillets in two-thirds of the marinade and set aside for a minimum of 2 hours. Place the vegetables in one-third of the marinade and set aside until ready to build your dish.

In a medium-sized bowl, mix the cooked rice with the buckwheat and tea leaves. Fold the nori sheet in half to break it into 2 even sheets. Line both sheets with the buckwheat rice.

Heat the grill to hot.

Place the gurnard on an oven tray and grill until the skin is caramelised.

Place the gurnard on top of the rice. Finish by carefully placing a neat pile of marinated vegetables to the side of each piece of gurnard and add a grapefruit segment.

SILKEN TOFU AND WATERMELON GAZPACHO

PREP TIME
— 30 minutes + 2 hours
straining time + 30 minutes
for chilling

SERVES
— 6

*This recipe is my wife
Kelly's favourite summer
dish. Each year, at the
beginning of spring, I know
I will need to ensure I have
a variation of this gazpacho
on the menu for her.*

GAZPACHO
— 200 g fresh silken tofu
— ½ watermelon, chopped
— 60 ml (2½ fl oz) rice
vinegar
— 3 tablespoons mirin
— 1 cup fresh basil leaves
— ½ red chilli
— ½ punnet cherry tomatoes
— 4 drops chilli oil

TO SERVE
— ½ cup watermelon cubes
— ¼ cup halved cherry
tomatoes
— ¼ cup mixed fresh basil and
coriander leaves
— 1 green chilli, sliced

Drain the excess water from the tofu.

Place the watermelon, rice vinegar, mirin, basil leaves,
red chilli and cherry tomatoes in a food processor and
purée until smooth. Pour the purée into a piece of muslin
suspended over a bowl and hang for 2 hours until all
the clear juice has run out. Add the chilli oil and chill the
clear gazpacho.

Once the gazpacho is chilled, cut the tofu into cubes and
divide among serving bowls. Pour the gazpacho over and
top with watermelon cubes, cherry tomato halves, herbs
and sliced green chilli.

ISHI YAKI
SALMON BELLY

COOK TIME
— 30 minutes

SERVES
— 2 sharing

Ishi yaki is a very old and traditional form of cooking on hot, dry stones. It is both a fun way to present a lovely belly of salmon and the stone imparts a distinctive terroir flavour through the fish. I serve this with my cucumber chilli pickle (see page 76).

— 1 hot stone for cooking
— 3 tablespoons sake
— 4 teaspoons soy sauce
— 3 tablespoons mirin
— 80 ml (2½ fl oz) dashi (see page 209)
— 1 teaspoon chilli garlic sauce
— freshly cracked black pepper
— 1 x 150 g salmon belly, boned

Preheat the oven to 200°C (400°F). Place the hot stone in the oven for about 20 minutes to get completely hot. You can substitute the stone for an ovenproof frying pan. This dish is served at the table while it is cooking on the hot stone.

Combine the sake, soy sauce, mirin, dashi, chilli garlic sauce and pepper to make the spiced basting sauce.

Run the salmon through the sauce and then place the belly directly onto the stone. Serve with a side bowl of the cucumber pickle.

ICEBERG SALAD WITH ROASTED ONION AND APPLE SOY DRESSING

PREP TIME
— 10 minutes + 30 minutes
  chilling time

SERVES
— 4 sharing

Iceberg is the most under-rated lettuce in the world. I think it's the best: it has texture, crunch, juice and holds up to almost anything you put with it. We always use iceberg at home and often whip this salad up as a crowd-pleaser on the side.

— 1 iceberg lettuce
— 2 medium-sized white onions, finely diced
— 1 celery stalk, finely diced
— 1 medium-sized carrot, finely diced
— ½ Granny Smith apple, skin on, grated
— 20 g (¾ oz) caster sugar
— 200 ml (7 fl oz) soy sauce
— 100 ml (3½ fl oz) olive oil
— 1 teaspoon sesame oil
— 150 ml (5 fl oz) rice vinegar
— 1 pinch nori matchsticks

Peel any outer leaves off the lettuce, discarding those that have cracked and discoloured. Use a small knife to cut out the core of the lettuce. This will allow the leaves to peel away easily.

Place the lettuce with the core down in a bowl of iced water and chill in the fridge for about 30 minutes. The lettuce will soak up the iced water and become really crispy and juicy.

Make the dressing by frying the diced onion in a frying pan over a medium heat until browned and soft. Add the celery, carrot and apple, and stir through to soften. Add the caster sugar and stir to dissolve. Then add the soy sauce, olive oil, sesame oil and rice vinegar. Stir, then allow to cool and incorporate the flavours.

Shake the excess water off the lettuce and peel the leaves off, keeping them nice and big. Spoon over the dressing and build up your salad in a serving bowl. Top with the nori matchsticks and serve.

KINGFISH SASHIMI SALAD WITH YUZU AND TRUFFLE DRESSING

PREP TIME
— 10 minutes

SERVES
— 2 sharing

This is a super-simple dish that is packed with loads of flavour. You can easily swap the kingfish out for any white fish. The truffle brings an earthy, umami element to the dish.

— 1 teaspoon garlic paste
— 1 tablespoon yuzu juice
— 1 tablespoon soy sauce
— 25 ml (¾ fl oz) mirin
— 30 ml (1 fl oz) truffle oil
— freshly cracked black pepper
— 200 g (7 oz) kingfish fillet, cut into 20 slices
— 1 small courgette, thinly sliced into rings
— 1 handful mixed salad leaves

Combine the garlic paste, yuzu juice, soy sauce, mirin, truffle oil and pepper to make your dressing.

Lay the sliced kingfish across your plate, add the courgette, spoon over the dressing and top with mixed salad. Serve.

SPINACH SALAD
WITH MAPLE SOY DRESSING

PREP TIME
— 15 minutes

SERVES
— 4 sharing

I remember when Darren and I were working through the opening menu for Masu. I had planned a more traditional version of this dish, called horenso oshitashi and using spinach and sesame. Darren was adamant that this contemporary version was better. After a lot of discussion, we ran with Darren's version which is the recipe here. To his credit it is now both one of my favourite salads on the menu and a best-seller. Hats off to Darren!

MAPLE SOY DRESSING
— 100 ml (3½ fl oz) olive oil
— 1 teaspoon shichimi pepper
— 30 ml (1 fl oz) lemon juice
— 20 ml (½ fl oz) rice vinegar
— 50 ml (1½ fl oz) maple syrup
— 100 ml (3½ fl oz) soy sauce
— 2 tablespoons honey

SALAD
— 1 ruby grapefruit, cut into segments
— 1 tablespoon caster sugar
— 1 bunch baby spinach leaves
— 1 teaspoon black sesame seeds
— 1 tablespoon garlic chips (see page 208)

To make this super-simple dressing, put all the ingredients in a medium-sized bowl and whisk to combine. You are not emulsifying, so you will need to give it a stir again before serving.

Place your grapefruit onto a metal baking tray or pan. Sprinkle with the caster sugar and use a blowtorch to caramelise the sugar to give you a delicious bittersweet balance with the grapefruit.

Build your salad in a large bowl, layering the spinach with grapefruit through it. Stir your dressing and coat the salad with it. Finish with a sprinkle of black sesame seeds and garlic chips.

CLOUDY BAY CLAMS
TOBAN YAKI

COOK TIME
— 10 minutes + 30 minutes
soaking time

SERVES
— 2 sharing

In my days working for Nobu Matsuhisa in London we served many, many toban; now I'm home I've made my own interpretation of this dish using some of the best New Zealand produce. A toban is a ceramic pot designed to capture all the steam and aroma.

— 12 Cloudy Bay clams
— 2 tablespoons unsalted butter
— 2 tablespoons sake
— 1 tablespoon soy sauce
— 1 tablespoon lemon juice
— 1 teaspoon ichimi chilli
— 1 tablespoon finely sliced ginger

Soak the clams in water for half an hour, to ensure they are fully purged of all sand and grit.

Heat a toban over a very high heat and add the clams directly to it. They will bounce and sizzle as they begin to release their juices. Reduce the heat, cover with a lid and cook for a further 2 minutes. Once all the clams have opened, add the butter, sake, soy sauce, lemon juice, ichimi chilli and ginger directly into the toban and cover again for 1 minute. It should really sizzle and bubble.

Serve immediately, removing the lid at the table so all of the aromas and sizzle are right there for your guests to enjoy.

SPICY MISO CRAYFISH TACOS WITH TOASTED SESAME SLAW

— 200 ml (7 fl oz) rice bran oil
— 6 gyoza wrappers

TOASTED SESAME SLAW
— ¼ cup finely sliced white cabbage
— ¼ cup finely sliced red cabbage
— ¼ cup finely sliced carrot
— 4 sprigs fresh coriander leaves
— 1 teaspoon toasted sesame seeds
— 2 tablespoons sushi vinegar
— 1 tablespoon rice bran oil

TO ASSEMBLE
— 3 tablespoons sweet white miso paste
— 1 teaspoon Korean hot pepper paste (gochujang)
— zest and juice of 1 lemon
— 120 g (4¼ oz) cooked crayfish tail, shell removed
— ¼ ripe avocado

COOK TIME
— 30 minutes

MAKES
— 6 tacos

I served a version of this at Nobu in London. Owner Nobu Matsuhisa has been a great inspiration to me over my culinary career.

Heat the oil to about 180ºC (350ºC).

Shallow-fry the wrappers, one at a time, until they begin to crisp up and stop bubbling. Remove from the oil and drain. While they are still warm, carefully fold them into a cup shape over a wooden spoon and allow to cool. You must work with the wrappers while they are warm, as when they cool they become hard.

To make the slaw, mix the cabbages and carrot with the coriander, toasted sesame seeds, sushi vinegar and rice bran oil.

Mix the white miso, hot pepper paste and some lemon zest and juice to make a quick paste. Pull the crayfish tail into small pieces, then mix the crayfish with the paste.

Blitz the avocado to a smooth purée and add some lemon zest and juice for flavour and to stop the avocado from discolouring.

Now build your tacos. Add a spoon of avocado purée to a taco cup, then a layer of pulled crayfish and top with the sesame slaw.

SOFT-SHELL CRAB AND AVOCADO TACO

COOK TIME
— 30 minutes

MAKES
— 6 tacos

The taco is a great way to carry flavour in a punchy bite-size form. I love the crispy, crunchy legs popping out of this taco.

— 200 ml (7 fl oz) rice bran oil
— 6 wheat gyoza wrappers

SLAW
— ½ cup finely sliced red cabbage
— ¼ cup finely sliced carrot
— ½ cup fresh coriander leaves
— 1 tablespoon rice vinegar
— ½ tablespoon mirin
— ½ tablespoon olive oil

TO ASSEMBLE
— ¼ ripe avocado
— juice of 1 lemon
— sea salt and freshly cracked black pepper
— 3 soft-shell crabs (can be replaced with 6 tiger prawns)
— 1 tablespoon potato starch

Heat the rice bran oil to about 180°C (350°F).

Shallow-fry the gyoza wrappers, one at a time, until they begin to crisp up and stop bubbling. Remove the wrappers from the oil and, while they are still hot, shape over a wooden spoon into a crisp taco shell. You must work with the wrappers while they are warm, as when they cool they become hard.

Keep the oil on the heat for cooking the crab.

Combine the sliced red cabbage and carrot with the coriander, rice vinegar, mirin and olive oil to make a bright and tasty Asian slaw.

In a food processor, purée the avocado with the lemon juice to form a smooth paste. Season with salt and pepper.

Halve the soft-shell crabs and pat dry. Dust the crabs in potato starch and cook until golden and crispy, 3-4 minutes, in the hot rice bran oil. Drain.

Build your tacos. The first layer is a heavy spoonful of avocado spread across the base of the taco, then a layer of Asian slaw and finish with half a crab in each taco. Serve hot.

KINGFISH CEVICHE TACO

— 200 ml (7 fl oz) rice bran oil
— 6 gyoza wrappers

TOASTED SESAME SLAW
— ¼ cup finely sliced white cabbage
— ¼ cup finely sliced red cabbage
— ¼ cup finely sliced carrot
— 4 sprigs fresh coriander leaves
— 1 teaspoon toasted sesame seeds
— 2 tablespoons sushi vinegar
— 1 tablespoon rice bran oil

TO ASSEMBLE
— 1 x 120 g (4¼ oz) kingfish fillet, cut into small dice
— 90 ml (3 fl oz) ceviche base (see page 204)
— ¼ ripe avocado
— zest and juice of 1 lemon

COOK TIME
— 20 minutes

MAKES
— 6 tacos

Another delicious version of our taco . . .

Heat the oil to about 180°C (350°F).

Shallow-fry the gyoza wrappers, one at a time, until they begin to crisp up and stop bubbling. Remove the wrappers from the oil and, while the wrappers are still warm, carefully fold them into a cup shape over a wooden spoon and allow to cool. You must work with the wrappers while they are warm, as when they cool they become hard.

To make the slaw, mix the sliced cabbages and carrot with the coriander, toasted sesame seeds, sushi vinegar and rice bran oil.

Place the diced kingfish in the ceviche base and allow to cure for a few minutes.

Blitz the avocado to a smooth purée and add the lemon zest and juice for flavour and to stop the avocado from discolouring.

Now build your tacos. Add a spoon of avocado purée to each taco shell, then a layer of the kingfish ceviche and top with sesame slaw.

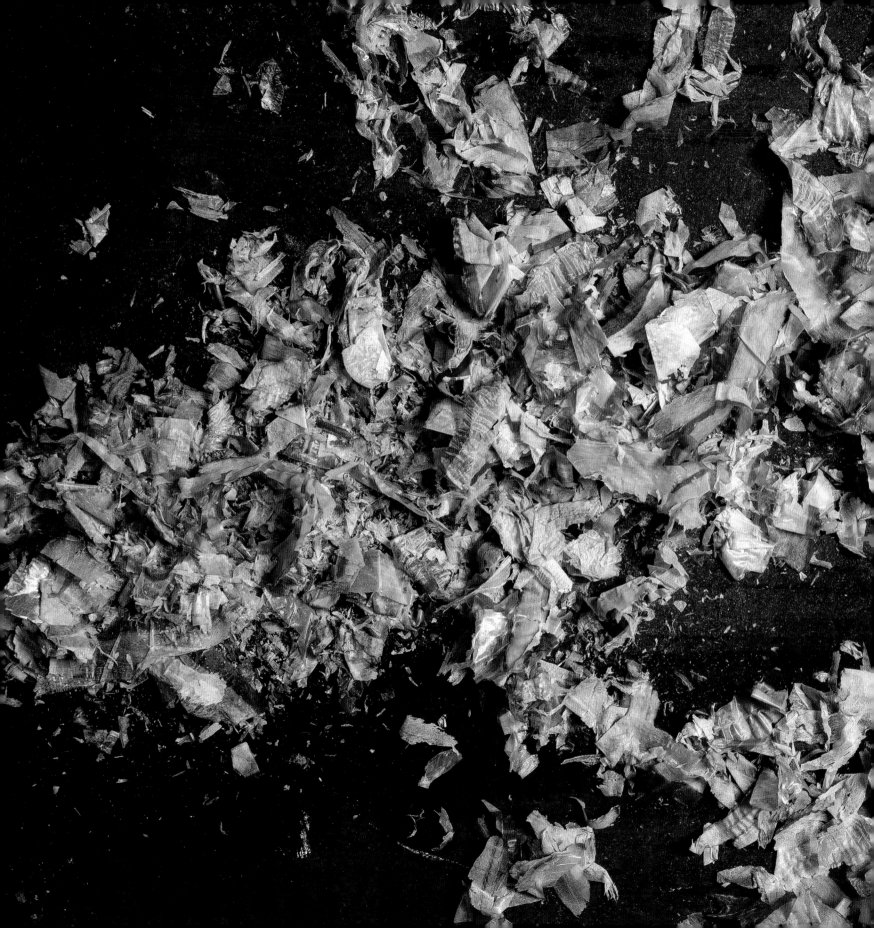

SOUP,
RICE AND
NOODLES

WHITE MISO SOUP WITH CLOUDY BAY CLAMS

COOK TIME
— 15 minutes + 30 minutes
  soaking time

SERVES
— 4

Enjoy restaurant-quality miso soup at home. You will need a coffee plunger for this one.

— 12 Cloudy Bay clams
— 3 tablespoons sweet white miso paste
— 2 dried shiitake mushrooms
— 1 x 10 cm (4 in) square dried kombu
— 1 handful bonito flakes
— 1 tablespoon soy sauce
— 800 ml (28 fl oz) filtered boiling water
— 2 pinches sliced spring onion to serve

Soak the clams in water for half an hour, to ensure they are fully purged of all sand and grit.

Place the white miso, shiitake, kombu, bonito flakes and soy sauce in the coffee plunger. Pour in the boiling water and give it a good stir to allow the miso to dissolve. Leave to steep for about 7 minutes. Give the miso one last stir, then press the coffee plunger down gently.

In a small saucepan, heat the clams until they just start to open, then pour over the hot miso soup and bring to a simmer. Remove from the heat when the clams have opened.

Serve in soup cups, scattered with sliced spring onion.

RED MISO SOUP
WITH SHIITAKE AND ENOKI MUSHROOMS

COOK TIME
— 20 minutes

SERVES
— 4

When you are working with red miso, you have to be mindful of the strength of flavour. Red miso has a very strong yeast flavour and, like Marmite and Vegemite, you only need a little. You need a coffee plunger for this soup.

— 2 tablespoons red miso paste
— 1 tablespoon sweet white miso paste
— 2 dried shiitake mushrooms
— 1 x 10 cm (4 in) square kombu
— 1 handful dried bonito flakes
— 1 tablespoon soy sauce
— 800 ml (28 fl oz) filtered boiling water

TO SERVE
— 4 little-finger-size bundles enoki mushrooms
— 4 little-finger-size strips toasted nori
— 4 fresh shiitake mushrooms
— 4 daikon tops

Place the red and white miso pastes, dried shiitake, kombu, bonito flakes and soy sauce into a coffee plunger. Pour in the boiling water and give it a good stir around to allow the miso to dissolve. Allow to steep for about 7 minutes, before giving it one last stir. Plunge the coffee press down gently.

Wrap each enoki mushroom bundle with a strip of nori. Wet the end of the nori with a damp finger so it sticks together.

Warm the miso soup in a small saucepan. Add the shiitake mushrooms and lightly poach for about 1 minute. Pour the soup and mushrooms into your serving cups and top with the enoki bundles and daikon tops.

SCAMPI, MISO AND MUSHROOM
KETTLE SOUP

COOK TIME
— 10 minutes

SERVES
— 2 sharing

This is a great autumn dish when mushrooms are out in their full glory. You can easily swap the oyster mushrooms for enoki or button. The soup can be drunk from ceramic cups and the scampi and mushrooms can be lifted out of the kettle with chopsticks. If you don't have a kettle, then use a saucepan.

— 600 ml (21 fl oz) dashi (see page 209)
— 3 tablespoons sweet white miso paste
— 4 scampi, shelled and veined
— 4 oyster mushrooms
— 3 drops chilli oil
— 1 pinch daikon leaves

Heat the dashi in a small saucepan and whisk in the white miso. Add the trimmed scampi and oyster mushrooms and allow them to poach for about 3 minutes.

Transfer the mixture to your kettle and bring back to just before boiling. Then add the chilli oil and daikon leaves and serve immediately.

UNAGI (FRESH-WATER EEL) DONBURI

COOK TIME
— 30 minutes

SERVES
— 1

Donburi are complete hunger-busters; that's the reason why they are a staple Japanese lunch item. Teriyaki eel is one of my favourites and I used to have a little donburi spot inside my local train station where they served the best donburi in Tokyo – according to me, anyway.

— 1 freshwater eel
— 100 ml (3½ fl oz) seafood teriyaki sauce (see page 202)
— 1½ cups cooked sushi rice (see page 206)
— 1 tablespoon red onion pickle (see page 208)
— 1 pinch fresh micro coriander leaves
— 1 fresh shiso leaf
— 1 pinch togarashi

Heat the grill or barbecue to hot.

Remove the back fat and skin from the eel by making a small cut in the tail and pulling the skin and fat away from the meat.

Brush the eel with your seafood teriyaki and heat it over the grill. We cook ours over the robata charcoal to give it a great smoky flavour. Once the eel is hot and caramelised, after around 5 minutes, it's time to build your donburi.

Place your rice in your bowl, add a small drizzle of the seafood teriyaki, place the grilled eel on top and serve with the red onion pickle, coriander leaves, shiso leaf and togarashi.

ROASTED RICE
KIRITANPO

COOK TIME
— 20 minutes

MAKES
— 2 skewers

This is a seriously delicious way to eat rice, and gets the kids asking for more . . . and more . . .

— 2 cups cooked sushi rice (see page 206)
— 2 tablespoons ginger juice
— olive oil for brushing
— ¼ cup chopped chives
— 3 tablespoons Kewpie mayonnaise to serve

Soak 4 wooden skewers in water.

Heat the barbecue to hot.

Take half of the cooked rice and mush to a coarse paste. Add the remaining rice and ginger juice, and form into sausage-like logs.

Place on the soaked wooden skewers and brush with a little oil.

Cook over the barbecue until the rice gets a nice golden edge. Sprinkle with chopped chives and serve hot with mayonnaise.

SOUP, RICE AND NOODLES

MASU

GREEN TEA AND BUCKWHEAT SOBA NOODLES WITH CRAYFISH

COOK TIME
— 30 minutes + 30 minutes resting time

SERVES
— 4 sharing

This fresh and lively dish is traditionally made during summer, as the noodles are served cold and chilled. The noodles can be made gluten free if you replace the plain flour with additional buckwheat – just be careful as the dough becomes very chalky and a little more difficult to work with. You will need a pasta machine for the noodles.

BUCKWHEAT NOODLES
— 130 g (4¾ oz) buckwheat flour
— 225 g (8 oz) plain flour
— 2 teaspoons green tea powder
— 125 ml (4 fl oz) cold water
— 1 tablespoon sesame oil

SOBA SAUCE
— 250 ml (9 fl oz) dashi (see page 209)
— 2 tablespoons mirin
— 1 tablespoon sake
— 2 tablespoons soy sauce

TO ASSEMBLE AND SERVE
— 2 cooked crayfish tails
— 1 tablespoon Korean hot pepper paste (gochujang)
— juice of 1 lemon
— ½ punnet cherry tomatoes, halved
— ½ ripe avocado, sliced
— 2 tablespoons salmon roe
— 1 pinch fresh micro coriander leaves
— 1 pinch finely chopped red chilli
— ¼ cup edible flowers
— 1 teaspoon toasted sesame seeds

For the noodles, combine the buckwheat and plain flours with the green tea powder in a food processor. Add the water and blitz to form a crumbly dough.

Remove from the food processor and place on a lightly floured bench. Knead for 10 minutes until smooth. Shape the dough into a ball and wrap in cling film. Refrigerate for 30 minutes.

Use a pasta machine to roll the dough into long even sheets. Lightly dust with flour and cut the dough into wedges. Start by running the dough through the widest setting and keep rolling until you reach setting number five. The sheets will become thinner and longer. Fit the noodle or spaghetti attachment to your machine. Run the sheets through to form your noodles. Dust with a little flour and leave to rest while you bring a saucepan of lightly salted water to the boil.

Blanch the noodles for about 2 minutes and transfer immediately to iced water. Allow to cool for 1 minute, then remove the noodles from the water and lightly rub in the sesame oil to stop them sticking together. Place the oiled noodles in the fridge.

For the soba sauce, combine the dashi, mirin, sake and soy sauce, and chill in the fridge.

For the crayfish, cut or lightly tear the crayfish tail meat into small, bite-size pieces. Mix with the hot pepper paste and lemon juice.

Place the chilled noodles into four serving bowls, top with crayfish, cherry tomato halves, avocado, coriander leaves, salmon roe, chilli and flowers, and sprinkle over the sesame seeds. Pour the cooled soba sauce over.

YAKISOBA
SOY CHICKEN EGG NOODLES

COOK TIME
— 10 minutes

SERVES
— 1

When I was living in Japan I went on a road trip with my friends to Mount Fuji. We found a small park at the base of the mountain where all the locals were picnicking. We fired up our little barbecue with a hot plate and cooked this for the six of us - this dish will always take me straight back to that day.

YAKISOBA SAUCE
— ⅓ cup ketchup
— 3 tablespoons Worcestershire sauce
— 1 tablespoon soy sauce
— 2 teaspoons Dijon mustard
— freshly cracked black pepper

NOODLES
— 2 tablespoons rice bran oil
— 2 skinned, boned chicken thighs, sliced
— ⅔ cup Chinese cabbage, shredded
— ½ cup bean sprouts
— ½ white onion, finely sliced
— 100 g packet egg noodles
— 1 pinch ao nori (shredded seaweed)
— 2 pinches red ginger pickle

Prepare the sauce by whisking together the ketchup, Worcestershire and soy sauces, mustard and pepper in a small bowl.

Heat the rice bran oil in a wok over a high heat, add the sliced chicken thighs and cook until nicely coloured. Remove the chicken and set aside.

Now add the cabbage, bean sprouts and onion to the wok, and cook until just beginning to brown. Add more oil as needed. Stir in the noodles until warmed and separated throughout the veges. Add the chicken and toss to evenly combine, stirring in half of the sauce. Keep adding sauce to reach your desired flavour.

Serve in a bowl and top with ao nori and red ginger pickle.

FROM
THE FRYER

TIGER PRAWN AND COURGETTE FLOWER TEMPURA

COOK TIME
— 10 minutes

SERVES
— 4 sharing

Tempura prawns should always be straight like arrows, not curled like @ signs.

There are a few tricks to getting nice crispy tempura, the first being to never over-whisk your batter as this will stretch the gluten and result in a soggy finish. It should have a few lumps and bumps through it and be ice-cold.

Always shallow-fry, don't deep-fry, for a more even and consistent temperature and cooking.

TEMPURA
— 2 litres (70 fl oz) rice bran oil
— 4 tiger prawn tails
— 2 courgette flowers
— 70 g (2½ oz) tempura flour
— 125 ml (4 fl oz) iced water

DASHI SOY
— 125 ml (4 fl oz) dashi (see page 209)
— ⅛ cup (1 fl oz) soy sauce
— ⅛ cup (1 fl oz) mirin

Heat the rice bran oil in a saucepan to around 180°C (350°F).

Take your prawn tails and, using a small sharp knife, carefully score the belly about a third of the way through at 2-mm intervals. The cuts should be on the inside curve of the prawns. Roll the prawns over and carefully push and stretch the prawns straight. Place your straight prawns in the fridge until needed.

Halve the courgette flowers and remove the stamens. Place in the fridge with the prawn tails until needed.

To make the tempura batter, place your tempura flour in a medium-sized mixing bowl. Use chopsticks or a fork to whisk in the iced water until you have a thin batter that runs off your fingers in 3 seconds. You don't want a thick, heavy batter but it should have a few lumps and bumps.

Run your prawns through the batter to give them a light coating and carefully place them in the hot oil to begin crisping up and cooking. We are starting with the prawns as they take the longest to cook. Follow immediately with the courgette flowers. With your fingers, flick some batter across the top of the prawns and flowers. This technique is called hana (meaning 'flower') and creates those delicious crispy edges. Cook until crisp but not golden, approximately 2½–3 minutes.

Remove the prawns and courgette flowers and drain for 1 minute on absorbent paper.

Combine the dashi, soy sauce and mirin in a saucepan, and warm.

Build a nice crispy salad, playing with the heights of the prawns and flowers. Serve with warm dashi soy.

YELLOW-BELLY FLOUNDER, CHILLI DAIKON AND LEMON

COOK TIME
— 15 minutes

SERVES
— 2 sharing

These crispy fish bones go great with cold beer. I remember eating them with dried squid as an early introduction to Japanese cuisine. These are the Japanese version of bar snacks and a nice change from peanuts.

— 1 x medium yellow belly flounder
— 75 g (2½ oz) plain flour
— 1 egg yolk
— 125 ml (4 fl oz) milk
— 15 g masago
— 60 g (2¼ oz) panko breadcrumbs
— rice bran oil for shallow-frying
— ¼ cup grated daikon
— 1 tablespoon momiji oroshi (chilli sauce)
— 1 lemon, halved

Fillet and skin the flounder. Remove the head and fins and keep the main skeleton to crisp up later. Trim the fillets into nice long fish fingers.

Lightly dust the fish fingers in the flour.

Mix the egg yolk and milk together in a small bowl to form an egg wash. Pass each dusted fish finger through the egg wash and then coat in the masago and panko breadcrumbs. Make sure all of the fingers are evenly coated in breadcrumbs. Set aside.

Heat the oil to 180°C (350°F).

In a saucepan big enough to hold the whole flounder skeleton, add enough water to cover the whole skeleton and bring to the boil. Add the flounder bones and cook for 2 minutes. Remove the bones from the hot water and wash under cold running water, removing all of the cooked meat and leaving cleaned white bones only. Pat dry and set aside.

Mix the grated daikon and momiji oroshi in a small bowl.

Cook the flounder bones in the hot oil until golden and crispy, then take them out of the oil and, while still warm, carefully form the bones into a curved bowl shape. Hold in position for a minute – they will harden into place while they cool. Place on a serving plate.

Cook the flounder fingers in the same hot oil until golden and crispy. Remove and drain on absorbent paper. Build the cooked fish fingers in the crispy fish-bone frame. Serve with the chilli daikon and half a lemon.

WEST COAST
WHITEBAIT
FRITTER

COOK TIME
— 10 minutes

SERVES
— 6 sharing

I remember catching whitebait at night on Kawau Island when I was a kid. We used to get tubs of whitebait in a few scoops of the net. In those days it was one egg to one cup of whitebait to make the purest of fritters. Today I like a little boost to the flavour and bling them out with the shichimi pepper and lime . . . Not sure what Mum thinks of this version, but I think it's a simple and super-delicious way to serve whitebait.

— 500 ml (17 fl oz) rice bran oil
— ½ cup whitebait
— 2 tablespoons potato starch
— ½ teaspoon shichimi pepper
— 1 green chilli, sliced to serve
— zest of 1 Tahitian lime to serve
— lime cheeks to serve

Heat the rice bran oil in a medium-sized saucepan to 180°C (350°F).

Mix your whitebait with the potato starch and shichimi pepper in a medium-sized bowl.

Drop the whitebait into the hot oil and fry quickly until crisp and it separates into individual whitebait.

Serve immediately with sliced green chilli, lime zest and lime cheeks.

COOKING WITH
CHARCOAL

EGGPLANT WITH GINGER MISO AND SESAME

Combine the sake and mirin in a small saucepan on a high heat and flame off the alcohol. Add the diced ginger and caster sugar and reduce by half.

Add the miso and ginger juice, and cook gently for a couple of minutes to evenly incorporate the miso with the liquid. Allow to cool at room temperature.

Halve the eggplants lengthways and score the flesh a few times in a criss-cross pattern – this allows the heat to get inside.

Heat the oil in a frying pan over a high heat. Shallow-fry the eggplant until golden, then drain on absorbent paper and allow to cool.

This is best finished over charcoal on your barbecue but can be done in the oven under the grill. Heat your barbecue or grill to hot.

Spoon and spread the ginger miso over the flat flesh side of the eggplant. Heat until the miso is just starting to bubble, then sprinkle with toasted sesame seeds and serve.

COOK TIME
— 30 minutes

SERVES
— 2

This is a really classic and simple Japanese miso dish. Served at many little local restaurants, it is a must-have with chicken yakitori. I have created several renditions of eggplant and miso, but find this ginger and barley miso combination to be the best.

— 100 ml (3½ fl oz) sake
— 100 ml (3½ fl oz) mirin
— 2 teaspoons diced ginger
— 1 teaspoon caster sugar
— 80 g (2¾ oz) barley miso paste
— 2 teaspoons pickled ginger juice
— 2 black Nadia eggplants
— vegetable oil for shallow-frying
— 2 teaspoons toasted sesame seeds

ROBATA ROAST CABBAGE WITH MISO MAYO

COOK TIME
— 10 minutes

SERVES
— 6 sharing

This recipe is a great way to bring cabbage onto the menu. The simple flavours of barbecued cabbage and mayo work for almost everyone's palate.

— 1 large Chinese cabbage
— 85 g (3 oz) salted butter, chopped
— 1 long mild red chilli, deseeded and sliced
— olive oil for brushing
— 4 tablespoons miso mayonnaise (see page 205)
— ito garashi (Japanese cayenne pepper threads)

Heat the barbecue to hot.

Trim the hard core from the cabbage and split the cabbage into quarters. Give them a good wash and set aside to allow the leaves to suck up some water.

Scatter the chopped butter over the cabbage, and add the chilli.

Brush the top and bottom of each piece with olive oil and roast over the barbecue for about 2–3 minutes on each side to allow for some nice caramelisation.

Serve with a side of miso mayo and garnish with ito garashi.

GRILLED ASPARAGUS,
PAN-FRIED QUAIL EGG AND SOY

COOK TIME
— 10 minutes

SERVES
— 2 sharing

There are so many ways to serve the humble asparagus, but if you look through the various cuisines you will often find it paired with egg. Here we use a quail egg, and soy sauce to add umami.

— 1 bunch green asparagus
— olive oil
— 1 quail egg
— 3 tablespoons sweet soy sauce

Heat the barbecue to hot.

It is really important to look after your asparagus; handle it gently or you will bruise it. Start by trimming the spikes off the spears back up to the head. Cut all the spears to one even length.

Blanch the asparagus for about 1½ minutes in a saucepan of salted boiling water. Remove and refresh in iced water until cool.

Rub the spears with olive oil and cook on the barbecue. You want to achieve a nice golden colour on the edges quite quickly.

At the same time, pan-fry your quail egg, sunny side up, in a small non-stick frying pan using a little of the oil.

To serve, pile the hot barbecued asparagus on a plate, drizzle over the sweet soy sauce and lay the quail egg on top.

BLACK COD IN CITRUS MISO

— 20 minutes + 24 hours
  marinating time

SERVES
— 2

*Black cod is a signature
dish at Masu. The
buttery, meaty flesh of the
black cod goes so well with
the charcoal flavours and
aromas. Whenever I have
guests at Masu I almost
always send them a black
cod dish.*

— 3 tablespoons sweet white
  miso paste
— 2 tablespoons lemon juice
— 1 tablespoon grapefruit
  juice
— 2 tablespoons mirin
— 1 tablespoon sake
— 1 teaspoon soy sauce
— 1 teaspoon ginger juice
— 2 x 180 g (6 oz) cod fillets
— 2 hajikami (pickled ginger
  stems) to serve

Whisk the white miso, lemon and grapefruit juices,
mirin, sake, soy sauce and ginger juice together to make
a smooth, wet marinade.

Reserve a touch of the marinade to serve on the side.
Marinate the cod for about 24 hours to get the best result.

Heat the barbecue to hot.

Cook the cod on the barbecue for 15–20 minutes, allowing
the miso to caramelise and the edges of the fillets to
colour up. This gives a delicious bittersweet balance
to the flavours.

Once the cod is cooked through, serve with the hajikami
and the reserved marinade on the side.

CEDAR PLANK ROAST SALMON
WITH GRAPEFRUIT MISO

COOK TIME
— 20 minutes + 1 hour marinating time

SERVES
— 1

I have served versions of this dish in the best restaurants in London and at Huka Lodge. The cedar adds a beautiful aroma and flavour when cooking and serving.

— ½ cup sweet white miso paste
— 1 tablespoon soy sauce
— 1 tablespoon mirin
— 1 tablespoon sake
— ½ ruby grapefruit
— 1 x 160 g (5½ oz) salmon fillet, skin on, scaled and boned
— cedar plank for roasting
— Nic's cucumber chilli pickle to serve (see page 76)
— lemon cheek to serve

Whisk the white miso, soy sauce, mirin and sake in a medium-sized mixing bowl, incorporating all the ingredients to form a smooth paste.

Remove all of the skin and pith from the grapefruit and cut out the segments. Squeeze the remaining juice from the grapefruit over the miso mixture and whisk together to form a smooth, wet paste. Add in the grapefruit segments.

Place the salmon fillet, with the skin side down, on a tray and liberally spoon the marinade over the fillet. Cover and marinate in the fridge for a minimum of 1 hour.

Preheat your oven to 180ºC (350ºF).

Place your marinated salmon on the cedar plank, ready for roasting. Try to keep some of the grapefruit segments on the top of the fillet.

Roast the salmon on the cedar plank for about 12 minutes until the miso has caramelised and the salmon has almost cooked through.

Serve on the plank with the cucumber chilli pickle and a lemon cheek on the side.

KINGFISH
ANTICUCHO
SKEWERS

COOK TIME
— 10 minutes

SERVES
— 2 sharing

While I was travelling in Peru we came across anticucho restaurants serving all sorts of meat and fish. These restaurants were traditionally for peasants, so they had all the offal – heart, lungs, you name it. Today the flavours remain the same but the meat has improved somewhat . . .

— 1 x 200 g (7 oz) kingfish fillet, sliced into bite-size chunks
— 2 spring onions, sliced into 2 cm (¾ in) lengths
— 250 ml (9 fl oz) anticucho base (see page 202)
— lime cheeks to serve

Soak two wooden skewers in water.

Heat your barbecue to hot.

Skewer the kingfish pieces, placing a length of spring onion between each piece of fish.

Baste the skewers in the anticucho base and quickly cook over a high heat to get nice caramelised edges, about 3 minutes. Baste a couple of times while cooking.

Serve the skewers with lime cheeks.

ROBATA BARBECUE
SNAPPER FILLET ANTICUCHO

COOK TIME
— 20 minutes + 3 hours
  marinating time

SERVES
— 1

This dish combines a classic Kiwi ingredient, snapper, and a modern approach to Peruvian Japanese cuisine.

— 1 x 150 g (5 ½ oz) snapper fillet, skin on, scaled and boned
— 125 ml (4 fl oz) anticucho base (see page 202)
— ½ lemon
— 1 cup cherry tomatoes
— 1 pinch celery heart leaves
— 1 pinch fresh basil tips
— 1 pinch shiso leaves

Marinate the snapper fillet in the anticucho base for about 3 hours.

Heat the barbecue to hot.

Thread two metal skewers through the snapper fillet on a diagonal as if you were sewing, ensuring the skewers cross over each other in an X to support the fillet once it is cooked.

Place the snapper, flesh side down, on the heat and cook until the fish begins to turn golden and the marinade caramelises. Turn once and cook the skin until crispy. Once cooked, 4-5 minutes, squeeze lemon juice over and place the fillet on your serving plate. Twist the skewers out if wished.

Use a blowtorch to sear the tomato skins. Halve the tomatoes and mix with celery heart, basil and shiso. Serve on the side of the snapper fillet.

CHARCOAL-GRILLED PIPERS
WITH LIME SEA SALT

COOK TIME
— 10 minutes

SERVES
— 6 sharing

Pipers remind me of my childhood. Whenever we went out whitebaiting they'd come in to feed, swimming past our light. We would just hit them with an old coat hanger to stun them and then catch them.

The simplicity of this dish with a cold beer on a summer's day is a real treat.

— 3 whole pipers, heads on, gutted
— olive oil for brushing
— 3 tablespoons sea salt
— 3 tablespoons lime zest
— 1½ limes
— 6 x 10 cm (4 in) squares muslin

This recipe is best cooked over charcoal. Heat your barbecue to hot.

Brush the pipers with olive oil. Rub the sea salt and lime zest together.

Lift the small fins and tails of the pipers and give them a liberal rub with the lime salt. This will help them to stand up and get great crispy edges.

Use a small knife to make a tiny cut in the front of the tail, twist each piper around and poke the long nose through the hole to form a circle.

Cook on the barbecue for about 4 minutes, turning only once.

Serve with a lime half wrapped in muslin.

CHICKEN
YAKITORI

COOK TIME

— 30 minutes

MAKES

— 6

There are thousands of yakitori restaurants in Japan, some seating as few as six customers. They serve chicken thighs, hearts, gizzards, skin – almost every part of the chicken can be skewered and cooked over charcoal. I have fond late-night memories of sipping sake and eating the many variations of chicken skewers in the back alleys of Tokyo.

— 2 skinned and boned chicken thighs, cut into bite-size pieces
— 1 spring onion, sliced into 2 cm (¾ in) lengths
— 200 ml (7 fl oz) teriyaki sauce (see page 202)
— 1 teaspoon shichimi pepper

Soak six wooden skewers in water.

Heat your charcoal barbecue until the embers are hot.

Thread a piece of chicken thigh followed by a length of spring onion onto the skewers. Repeat twice, finishing with a piece of chicken.

Dip your chicken skewers in the teriyaki sauce and cook over the embers – you want the sauce to colour up and caramelise. Dip again and turn your skewers. Repeat three times to get a great glaze on the skewers.

Season with shichimi pepper and serve.

BARBECUED
CHICKEN WINGS

COOK TIME
— 20 minutes

SERVES
— 2 sharing

When I was working in Tokyo, after a very long hard day in the kitchen I would go to a yakitori bar that had been around since the 1920s and have an ice-cold beer and eat charcoal-grilled chicken wings much like these ones . . . This is classic izakaya cuisine.

— 6 chicken wings
— 200 ml (7 fl oz) chicken marinade (see page 204)
— 1 pinch sea salt
— 1 pinch shichimi pepper

Soak six wooden skewers in water.

Heat the barbecue to hot.

Trim the wing tips from the chicken and save for making stock. Score the back of the remaining wings. Skewer each wing lengthways and place in the marinade, ready to grill.

Grill the wings over the open flame, basting regularly with the marinade until cooked and the edges have caramelised, 8–10 minutes.

Serve with a pinch of sea salt and shichimi pepper.

BABY BACK **RIBS**

MASTER STOCK
— 2 litres (70 fl oz) water
— 100 ml (3½ fl oz) mirin
— 300 ml (10½ fl oz) soy sauce
— 1 tablespoon sliced ginger
— 1 tablespoon sliced garlic
— 1 orange, sliced
— 1 cinnamon quill
— 1 red chilli, split

— 2 x 350 g (12 oz) baby back pork rib racks

RIB GLAZE
— 250 ml (9 fl oz) hoisin sauce
— 125 ml (4 fl oz) soy sauce
— 200 ml (7 fl oz) mirin
— 200 ml (7 fl oz) sweet chilli sauce
— 2 tablespoons sesame seeds

— lime cheek to serve

COOK TIME
— 1 hour

SERVES
— 4

We serve this with hot towels to clean your hands, because there is only one way to eat ribs and that is with your hands.

This master stock is a great way to get the ribs super-soft and falling off the bone.

Combine all of the master stock ingredients in a medium-sized saucepan big enough to take the pork racks as well. Bring to a simmer, then turn down the heat. Add the ribs and lightly poach for about 40 minutes. Allow the ribs to cool in the stock.

In a medium-sized bowl, combine the rib glaze ingredients and whisk together.

Heat up your charcoal barbecue to hot.

Remove the ribs from the stock and cook on the hot grill, basting every couple of minutes with the glaze until you get a delicious glaze and the edges caramelise. This will take a good 12–15 minutes. Take care while glazing, as it will burn easily.

Serve hot with a lime cheek on the side.

WAGYU BEEF SIRLOIN, BONE MARROW AND SHIITAKE

COOK TIME
— 40 minutes

SERVES
— 2

Wagyu is the prized Japanese beef. The cows are at times fed with beer and massaged by hand – not a bad life for cattle.

The Waygu breed is genetically smaller with a slow growth rate. Wagyu beef can be eaten raw like sashimi, but in this recipe I have used sirloin and grilled it over the barbecue.

— 300 g (10½ oz) Wagyu beef sirloin
— sea salt and freshly cracked black pepper
— 4 fresh shiitake mushrooms, sliced
— 1 clove garlic, sliced
— 75 ml (2¼ fl oz) beef teriyaki sauce (see page 202)
— 1 x 12 cm (4½ in) beef marrow bone, split lengthways
— 1 fresh shiso leaf
— 1 nasturtium leaf

This beef is best cooked over charcoal, so give your coals enough time to heat up to hot.

Season your beef well with sea salt and freshly cracked black pepper.

In a small saucepan, poach your shiitake and garlic in the teriyaki sauce while you cook your beef.

Grill the beef on the barbecue for about 8-10 minutes on either side - this is a big steak and it will need some cooking time. Turn a few times so as not to darken the edges too much. Halfway through the cooking time, roast your bone marrow on the barbecue until the marrow has started to become clear and a little wobbly.

Allow your beef to rest for 10 minutes before serving.

Place the poached shiitake and garlic over the marrow bone and top with a fresh shiso leaf and nasturtium leaf.

BARBECUED PORK BELLY, HOT PEPPER MISO AND CHARRED CHINESE CABBAGE

COOK TIME
— 1 hour + 2–24 hours
marinating time

SERVES
— 4

We don't eat much pork belly at home, but this version with miso and hot pepper is really tasty. This recipe also works very well with salmon and chicken.

This recipe calls for a bit of time, as the pork belly really benefits from 24 hours in the marinade – but if you don't have the time a minimum of 2 hours will do.

PORK BELLY
— 5 tablespoons Korean hot pepper paste (gochujang)
— 3 tablespoons sweet white miso paste
— 90 ml (3 fl oz) lemon juice
— 3 tablespoons mirin
— 2 tablespoons sake
— 750 g (1 lb 10 oz) pork belly

CHARRED CHINESE CABBAGE
— 1 Chinese cabbage
— 60 ml (2 fl oz) mirin
— 90 ml (3 fl oz) soy sauce
— 60 ml (2 fl oz) good-quality olive oil

Make the marinade by combining the hot pepper paste with the white miso, lemon juice, mirin and sake. Whisk together to form a smooth, wet paste.

Trim the pork belly to neaten up the shape and edges. With a sharp knife, neatly score the top of the belly to allow the marinade to penetrate past the skin. Cover the pork belly in the marinade and refrigerate for 2 24 hours.

On the day you want to cook the pork belly, peel off any dry or brown cabbage leaves. Cut the cabbage into six long wedges – the base core will hold each wedge together. Mix the mirin, soy sauce and olive oil together and pour it over the cabbage.

Heat your charcoal barbecue to hot.

Pork belly is best cooked as a whole piece. Cook it slowly over the embers so you get delicious rendered pork with caramelised miso-marinated edges. This will take at least 40 minutes.

Remove from the barbecue and allow the pork belly to rest for a good 10 minutes.

While it is resting, quickly cook the cabbage over a high heat, allowing the mirin and soy to darken up on the edges.

Serve the charred cabbage with the rested whole pork belly, or slice the belly to serve individually.

TERIYAKI BABY CHICKEN AND SHIITAKE RICE

COOK TIME
— 40 minutes

SERVES
— 2

This is a great dish. It brings together classic and simple teriyaki chicken and then dials it up into an elegant and refined dish, packed full of flavour. I like to make this as a lunch special at Masu and add my chilli cucumber pickle.

SHIITAKE RICE
— 1 teaspoon ginger paste
— 1 clove garlic
— 1 teaspoon mirin
— 1 teaspoon soy sauce
— 1 medium-sized shallot, finely chopped
— ½ cup cooked sushi rice (see page 206)
— ⅓ cup sliced fresh shiitake mushrooms

TERIYAKI CHICKEN
— 2 baby chickens, deboned
— 2 fresh shiso leaves
— 250 ml (9 fl oz) chicken teriyaki sauce (see page 202)
— 1 tablespoon shichimi pepper

Heat your barbecue to hot.

To a food processor, add the ginger paste, garlic, mirin and soy sauce. Purée until smooth, then add the finely chopped shallot.

Mix the cooked sushi rice and shiitake in a bowl, then add the garlic purée and mix until evenly combined. Shape into two neat balls.

Line the inside of the chickens with the shiso leaves, then add the seasoned rice balls. Roll together, putting the chickens back into shape, and tie up with butcher's twine.

Brush your baby chickens with teriyaki sauce. Grill and caramelise the chickens on the barbecue, turning and rolling regularly to ensure they cook evenly and the teriyaki doesn't burn. Baste with teriyaki sauce three or four times while cooking. The chicken will take about 20–25 minutes.

Allow to rest for about 5 minutes. Then carve off the drumsticks and slice the breast into even bite-size portions.

Season with shichimi pepper.

FAMILYMEALS

TEENAGE DATE-NIGHT
OKONOMIYAKI
SAVOURY PRAWN PANCAKE

COOK TIME
— 30 minutes

SERVES
— 2 sharing

Instant Japanese food at its best! In Japan, okonomiyaki cafés are filled with teenagers out on dates. In these cafés the tables have a hot-plate in the centre where you cook and eat your pancake together.

— 2 eggs
— 125ml (4 fl oz) water
— 90 g (3¼ oz) Japanese pancake flour (okonomiyaki flour)
— 4 cooked prawn tails, cut into bite-size chunks
— ½ cup finely sliced white cabbage, soaked in iced water
— ½ cup sliced spring onion
— olive oil for cooking
— Kewpie mayonnaise to serve
— tonkatsu sauce to serve
— 1 bunch fresh Vietnamese mint leaves to serve
— 1 bunch fresh coriander leaves to serve
— ½ mild long red chilli
— 1 handful bonito flakes to serve

Begin by whisking the eggs and water into the pancake flour to form a smooth batter.

Add the prawns to the batter with half of the sliced cabbage and the spring onion. Stir through the batter to evenly disperse the ingredients.

Heat a small frying pan over a medium heat, and add a dash of olive oil. Ladle in two even pancakes of the batter. Cook until the batter rises and you get a nice golden colour on the bottom. Once golden, flip and cook for a further few minutes until both sides are evenly coloured.

Remove the pancakes from the pan and place them on a serving plate.

Add a good loose drizzle of mayo and tonkatsu sauce. Drain the last of the cabbage and add to the pancakes. Top with the Vietnamese mint, coriander and bonito flakes, and serve.

LAMB LEG ROASTED WITH MASU HOT PEPPER SPICES

COOK TIME

— 2 hours 90 minutes +
  24 hours marinating time

SERVES

— 6

I first came across this Korean hot pepper paste at a small donburi restaurant in London, where they were serving it with fried chicken on top of rice. I have used it with all kinds of meat ever since. This lamb goes with any of the vegetable sharing dishes. The lamb leg is best spiked and marinated the day before.

— 1 x 2.5 kg (5 lb 8 oz) lamb leg
— freshly cracked black pepper
— 2 long fresh rosemary sprigs, finely chopped
— 8 tablespoons Korean hot pepper paste (gochujang)
— 3 tablespoons white wine
— 3 tablespoons mirin
— 2 tablespoons soy sauce
— 2 tablespoons freshly crushed garlic
— 1 tablespoon ginger paste
— juice of 1 lemon

Trim the top of the lamb shank to allow the meat to pull down while cooking and season with pepper.

Combine the rosemary, hot pepper paste, white wine, mirin, soy sauce, garlic, ginger paste and lemon juice in a medium-sized bowl and whisk to form a wet marinade.

Coat the lamb leg in the hot pepper marinade. Cover and store in the fridge overnight.

The next day, remove the lamb from the fridge and allow to stand for 1 hour at room temperature – this will ensure the lamb cooks more evenly.

Preheat your oven to 180ºC (350ºF).

Place your lamb leg on a roasting tray and cook for approximately 1 hour 15 minutes. Remove from the oven and rest the lamb for 20 minutes before carving.

BEEF SIRLOIN TERIYAKI WITH ROASTED RICE AND HERBS

COOK TIME
— 40 minutes + 1 hour marinating time

SERVES
— 6

When I am cooking at home for bigger groups of friends, I will often go to this recipe. It's simple to cook and the teriyaki and fresh herbs just jump on the palate. Serve with any of the vegetable sharing dishes.

BEEF TERIYAKI
— 1 x 1.2–1.5 kg (2 lb 12 oz– 3 lb 5 oz) beef sirloin
— sea salt and freshly cracked black pepper
— 250 ml (9 fl oz) beef teriyaki sauce (see page 202)

ROASTED RICE AND HERBS
— 1 cup sushi rice (see page 206)
— 500 ml (17 fl oz) vegetable oil
— 2 tablespoons chopped fresh Vietnamese mint
— 2 tablespoons chopped fresh parsley
— 2 tablespoons chopped fresh shiso leaves
— 60 g (2¼ oz) Korean dried chilli flakes

Trim the sirloin of all sinew, leaving a thin layer of fat across the top. Season heavily with salt and pepper.

Marinate the beef in half of the teriyaki sauce for an hour or so before cooking.

Heat your charcoal barbecue to hot.

Wash the rice and soak in water for 20 minutes. Then drain and allow to dry for 20 minutes.

In a medium-sized saucepan, heat the oil to just under smoking. Carefully put the washed rice into the hot oil. It will spit a little. Cook the rice until golden and crisp, about 1½ minutes. Drain and pat dry on absorbent paper and allow to cool.

Once the rice has cooled, give it a quick pound in a mortar and pestle to break it down a little. Add the fresh herbs and Korean dried chilli flakes.

Cook the beef over the open charcoal, basting regularly with the remaining teriyaki sauce to give it a dark caramelised finish. Cook to your liking: I think medium-rare, which will take about 20 minutes, is perfect for a larger joint of meat.

Remove from the barbecue and rest for 10 minutes. Then rest the beef on the rice and herb mix, and slice into nice thick steaks.

ALL
THINGS
SWEET

MASU CEDAR ROAST CHOCOLATE AND GREEN TEA PUDDING

COOK TIME
— 30 minutes

SERVES
— 6

The beautiful thing about this recipe is the flavour the cedar boxes put into the roasted chocolate. You will need six cedar boxes, or you can use ramekins. I serve this with ginger beer ice cream.

MOULDS
— 150 g (5½ oz) unsalted butter
— 220 g (7¾ oz) caster sugar

PUDDINGS
— 80 g (2¾ oz) cocoa butter
— 100 g (3½ oz) unsalted butter
— 265 g (9¼ oz) Valrhona chocolate (Guanaja 70%)
— 120 g (4¼ oz) honey
— 5 whole eggs
— 100 g (3½ oz) egg yolks
— 60 g (2¼ oz) egg whites
— 50 g (1¾ oz) caster sugar
— matcha green tea powder to serve

Preheat the oven to 180°C (350°F).

Begin by melting the butter for greasing the moulds – you can use cedar boxes or ramekins. Pour the hot butter into one mould at a time. Make sure all the sides are lined with butter, then pour into the next mould and repeat for all the moulds. Fill one mould at a time with the caster sugar and ensure all the sides and the base are lined with caster sugar. Then pour the sugar into the next mould and repeat until all the moulds are lined. Place in the fridge until required for filling.

For the puddings, melt the cocoa butter, butter, chocolate and honey over a double boiler.

Whisk the whole eggs and yolks together, and warm them up by whisking continuously over a double boiler. Once they have begun to fluff up, transfer them to a cake mixer and whisk until light and fluffy.

To make a meringue, combine the egg whites and caster sugar in a cake mixer and whisk to stiff peaks.

Fold the warm chocolate into the fluffy egg-yolk sabayon, then fold the meringue into the chocolate sabayon.

Fill the greased moulds to the top, then gently tap them on the bench to knock the air out of the puddings. Bake for 12 minutes.

Serve hot with a heavy dusting of matcha green tea powder.

HONEYCOMB AND PASSION FRUIT
CHAWAN MUSHI

COOK TIME
— 45 minutes + 2 hours
   setting time

SERVES
— 6

Chawan mushi is traditionally a savoury dish, a very soft baked custard usually made with either chicken or prawns. When flipped into a dessert, it makes a sensationally light baked cream. This is one of Kelly's all-time favourites and a staple on the menu. You can easily change the fruit topping according to what's seasonal.

— 165 ml (5¼ fl oz) liquid honey
— 165 ml (5¼ fl oz) cream
— 250 ml (9 fl oz) milk
— 250 ml (9 fl oz) coconut cream
— 5 egg yolks
— 5 whole eggs
— 3 tablespoons fresh honeycomb to serve
— 3 fresh passion fruit to serve
— 1 pinch sea salt to serve
— 1 tablespoon Nata de Coco to serve
— mint leaves to garnish

Preheat a convection oven to 80ºC (175ºF) or a conventional oven to 160ºC (315ºF).

Heat the honey and cream together in a saucepan over a medium heat. Allow to cool, then add the milk, coconut cream, yolks and whole eggs and whisk to a wet batter. Pass the mixture through a sieve.

Pour the chawan mushi into your serving bowls and steam-bake in the convection oven for about 40-45 minutes. Alternatively, place the serving bowls in a tray filled with enough water to come halfway up the sides of the bowls and bake in a conventional oven for 40-45 minutes. Allow to cool on the bench, then transfer to the fridge and allow to set – this will take around 2 hours.

Serve cold with a piece of fresh honeycomb, the pulp of half a passion fruit, nata de coco, mint leaves and a tiny pinch of salt.

GREEN TEA, BANANA AND HAZELNUT CRÈME BRÛLÉE

Preheat a convection oven to 80°C (175°F) or a conventional oven to 160°C (315°F).

Whisk together the whole eggs, egg yolks and green tea powder.

Blitz the coconut water and flesh together to form a smooth paste. Place the milk and coconut paste in a saucepan over a medium heat and bring to the boil. Remove from the heat and slowly add the hot milk to the egg mixture to cook the eggs. Pass through a fine sieve.

Pour into your serving bowls and steam-bake in a convection oven for about 25 minutes. Alternatively, place the serving bowls in a tray filled with enough water to come halfway up the sides of the bowls and bake in a conventional oven for 25 minutes. Allow to cool on the bench, then transfer to the fridge and allow to set – this will take around 2 hours.

Heat the sugar in a saucepan over a medium heat until a caramel forms. Skewer a hazelnut and dip it in the caramel. Hang it off the end of the bench so the caramel falls into a spear. Repeat with the remaining nuts and caramel.

Sprinkle the icing sugar over the sliced banana and caramelise with a blow torch. Serve the brûlée with the caramelised banana and hazelnut spear.

COOK TIME
— 30 minutes + 2 hours setting time

SERVES
— 6

One of my favourite desserts. My best mate in London, Julian, showed me this combination of green tea and banana and I've been sold ever since.

— 3 whole eggs
— 3 egg yolks
— 1 teaspoon matcha green tea powder
— 100 ml (3½ fl oz) fresh coconut water
— 100 g (3½ oz) fresh coconut flesh
— 390 ml (13½ fl oz) milk
— 100 g (3½ oz) caster sugar
— 6 hazelnuts
— 2 bananas, sliced
— icing sugar to serve

DRUNKEN
PINEAPPLE

COOK TIME

— 30 minutes + 1 hour
   marinating time

SERVES

— 4

*This drunken pineapple
takes the ingredients of a
classic piña colada and turns
them into a modern dessert.
When people ask me to bring
a plate to a barbecue, I often
bring this. No one expects to
be cooking pineapple like this
and it's a memorable way
to finish a great meal with
friends.*

— 1 ripe pineapple
— 110 g (3¾ oz) demerara
  sugar
— 250 ml (9 fl oz) dark rum
— juice of 1 lime
— 1 red chilli, sliced
— 125 ml (4 fl oz) umeshu
  (plum wine)
— ⅓ cup honey
— ⅓ cup fresh mint and basil
  tips
— 1 red chilli, finely chopped

This is best cooked over a barbecue, so get your coals hot.

Start by trimming off the pineapple skin, then cut the
flesh into quarters and trim out the core. You should end
up with four skinless and coreless sections of pineapple.

Now make the drunken basting sauce. Add the sugar,
rum, lime juice, chilli, umeshu and honey to a medium-
sized saucepan and heat to dissolve the sugar and
combine all the ingredients. Allow to cool.

Put the pineapple quarters in the drunken solution and
allow to marinate for 1 hour.

Place the marinated pineapple on the barbecue and grill,
getting some nice coloured edges and allowing the honey
to catch and caramelise.

Once cooked, slice the quarters into bite-size pieces and
brush with a little more marinade to keep the pineapple
shiny and fresh. Pile into bowls and scatter the fresh herb
tips and sliced red chilli across the top.

FROZEN SUMMER BERRIES, WHITE CHOCOLATE AND PASSION FRUIT

COOK TIME
— 20 minutes + time to freeze
the berries

SERVES
— 6

Who doesn't love berries and chocolate? This is my favourite crowd-pleaser recipe, and it's so easy to whip up at the end of a busy lunch or dinner with friends and family.

— 1 punnet raspberries
— 2 punnets strawberries
— 1 punnet blackberries
— 1 punnet blueberries
— 3 fresh passion fruit
— 1 bunch fresh mint sprigs
— 1 bunch fresh basil leaves
— 250 g (9 oz) white chocolate, broken into small pieces
— 60 ml (2 fl oz) umeshu (plum wine)
— 80 ml (2½ fl oz) cream
— matcha green tea powder to serve

Wash and trim the berries. I usually just halve any juicy big strawberries and leave everything else whole. Place the berries on a plate, not in a bowl, and freeze them. You want them to be individually frozen, not in a big lump.

Halve the passion fruit and pick the mint and basil down to the fine small tips.

Scatter the frozen berries across a serving plate, squeeze the passion fruit over the berries and sprinkle the mint and basil over.

Soften the chocolate and umeshu together in a double boiler. Add a little of the cream to get a beautiful pouring consistency. Transfer to a warm pouring jug.

By now the berries will be a soft iced texture. Present the berries at the table, pour the warm sauce over and listen to the ohhs and ahhhs. Dust with green tea powder and eat immediately for a hot chocolate with frozen berry sensation.

SESAME
MARSHMALLOW

COOK TIME
— 30 minutes

SERVES
— 4 sharing

*I used to love toasting
marshmallows beside the
campfire when I was a kid,
and I think almost everyone
has an affection for them.
We make this recipe on
occasion at the restaurant.
The memories it brings
back for our customers, and
their smiles, are amazing –
a really nice touch to finish
your night out.*

— 150 g (5 ½ oz) caster sugar
— 90 ml (3 fl oz) water
— 8 g gelatine powder
— 5 g agar
— 2 g sesame paste
— 2 tablespoons cornflour

Place the sugar, water and powdered gelatine in a small
saucepan and heat to 123°C on a sugar thermometer.
Add the agar and bring the heat up to 125°C. Whisk in
the sesame paste.

Dust a small tray with the cornflour and pour in the
marshmallow mixture. Allow to cool and cut into
matchbox-size pieces.

Skewer each sesame marshmallow and toast over
charcoal, as you would by the campfire.

WHITE MISO
SOUFFLÉS

COOK TIME

— 20 minutes

SERVES

— 6

Soufflés are tricky but well worth the effort. At Masu we cook these in bamboo ramekins as the mild toasted-wood flavour really complements the white miso. You can use traditional ceramic ramekins, but reduce the cooking time by about 2 minutes. Serve with vanilla ice cream.

— 4 teaspoons unsalted butter
— ½ cup sweet white miso paste
— 275 g (9¾ oz) caster sugar
— 6 whole eggs, separated
— 6 egg whites

Preheat your oven to 185°C (355°F).

Soften your butter and grease your soufflé dishes.

In a large mixing bowl, whisk together the white miso, ¼ cup of the caster sugar and the six egg yolks.

In a separate bowl beat the twelve egg whites until they foam. Then gradually add in the remaining sugar and whisk to soft peaks. Fold the whites into the miso mixture.

Fill your soufflé dishes, then tap them gently on the bench to ensure they have neat, flat tops.

Bake for 9-12 minutes until they have risen and just set.

WHITE MISO
PAVLOVA

COOK TIME
— 1 hour

SERVES
— 4 people sharing

I have always wanted to work a pavlova onto the Masu dessert menu, so I asked Sam, our pastry chef, to create something along those lines. Well, on the last day of photographing this book, she casually prepared this recipe; once I tasted her pavlova I knew it had to be part of the book. I can see this is going to become a signature dessert item – thanks, Sam.

PAVLOVA
— 70 g (2½ oz) egg whites
— 80 g (2¾ oz) caster sugar
— 1 tablespoon cornflour
— 2 tablespoons icing sugar
— splash of white vinegar
— ⅛ vanilla pod, split and seeds scraped out

WHITE MISO CUSTARD
— 125 ml (4 fl oz) milk
— 25 g (1 oz) caster sugar
— ¼ vanilla pod
— 25 ml (¾ fl oz) milk
— 45 g (1½ oz) egg yolks
— 2½ tablespoons caster sugar
— 1½ tablespoons cornflour
— 1 tablespoon sweet white miso paste
— ½ gelatine sheet
— 20 g (¾ oz) butter

Preheat the oven to 140°C (285°C). Line a baking tray with baking paper.

To make the pavlova, whisk the egg whites with a beater or in a cake mixer and slowly add the caster sugar. When they form soft peaks, add the cornflour and icing sugar, followed by the vinegar and vanilla. Whisk to combine.

Place in spoonfuls onto the lined tray and bake for about 35 minutes. Remove from the oven and allow to cool.

To make the custard, heat the first measure of milk and sugar with the vanilla pod in a saucepan.

Whisk the second measure of milk, egg yolks, second measure of sugar, cornflour and white miso to combine. Add to the hot milk and cook until the mixture comes to the boil. Remove from the heat.

Soften the gelatine sheet in cold water. Squeeze out excess water before using.

Whisk the softened gelatine and the butter into the custard base, then strain and cool.

Serve together . . . and be prepared to be asked for seconds.

BASE
RECIPES

ANTICUCHO BASE

Peru has the largest Japanese population outside of Japan, and over time the Peruvians and Japanese have beautifully combined their cuisines.

PREP TIME
— 5 minutes

MAKES
— 1 litre (35 fl oz)

— 450 ml (15½ fl oz) sake
— 250 ml (9 fl oz) rice vinegar
— 125 ml (4 fl oz) soy sauce
— 100 ml (3½ fl oz) lemon juice
— 25 g (1 oz) smoked dried chilli flakes
— ½ cup fresh basil leaves
— 2 tablespoons ground cumin
— 1 tablespoon garlic purée
— 250 ml (9 fl oz) olive oil

Combine the sake, rice vinegar, soy sauce and lemon juice together in a bowl.

Place the smoked chilli flakes, basil, cumin and garlic purée in a food processor and blitz to a paste with the olive oil.

Add the olive oil paste to the wet sake mix and stir together.

This antichucho base will keep for two weeks in the fridge.

TERIYAKI SAUCE

This is the base sauce for teriyaki; you can add either fish, chicken or beef for added complexity of flavour and increased umami.

You can keep this sauce in a preserving jar in your fridge – it's a great go-to sauce to have handy.

COOK TIME
— 1 hour

MAKES
— 500 ml (17 fl oz)

— 250 ml (9 fl oz) sake
— 250 ml (9 fl oz) mirin
— 75 g (2½ oz) caster sugar
— 2 pinches dried chilli flakes
— 250 ml (9 fl oz) soy sauce
— 125 g (4½ oz) roasted chicken frames, or beef or fish bones (see below)

Bring the sake and mirin to the boil in a saucepan over a medium heat and burn off the alcohol.

Add the caster sugar, chilli flakes and soy sauce to the mirin and simmer until it has reduced by half.

For a chicken, beef or fish base, add the roasted bones in with the sugar, and follow the method above. In addition you will need to skim the sauce once it's cooled to remove any fat deposits.

TO ROAST THE BONES
Preheat the oven to 180°C (350°F).

Place the bones in a roasting tray and roast for 40 minutes, turning every 10 minutes.

CEVICHE BASE

I fell in love with ceviche when I was travelling through Peru on a exploratory food trip some years ago. I knew of ceviche before we went, but there was a lot to discover about the leche de tigre –'tiger's milk' – the marinating sauce that is so important for really good ceviche. Tiger's milk is the liquid formed when the fish has been marinating for about 15 minutes. It's understanding exactly when the flavour of the tiger's milk is perfect that is important.

PREP TIME
— 5 minutes

MAKES
— 150–200 ml (5–7 fl oz)

— 100 ml (3½ fl oz) lime juice
— 50 ml (1½ fl oz) yuzu juice
— 15 ml (½ fl oz) soy sauce
— 1 teaspoon garlic paste
— 1 teaspoon ginger paste
— 1 teaspoon mirin
— 1 teaspoon dried chilli flakes
— 4 drops chilli oil
— 40 ml (1¼ fl oz) olive oil
— freshly cracked black pepper

Combine all of the ingredients and store in the fridge ready for use.

This sauce will keep for two weeks.

CHICKEN MARINADE

This recipe can be used to baste chicken wings on the barbecue, or a whole roast chicken cooked in the oven.

COOK TIME
— 10 minutes

MAKES
— 500 ml (17 fl oz)

— 20 g (¾ oz) ichimi chilli
— 50 ml (1½ fl oz) chilli oil
— 270 ml (9½ fl oz) sake
— 150 ml (5 fl oz) soy sauce
— 50 g (1¾ oz) ginger paste

Combine all of the ingredients in a saucepan and bring to a simmer over a medium heat.

Allow to cool and store in a jar in the fridge until ready to use.

This marinade will keep for two weeks.

BASIC MAYO

We use this mayonnaise base to build our wasabi mayonnaise, as well as many others.

PREP TIME
— 10 minutes

MAKES
— 500 ml (17 fl oz)

— 2 egg yolks
— ½ teaspoon English mustard
— 40 ml (1¼ fl oz) lemon juice
— 400 ml (14 fl oz) vegetable oil

Whisk the egg yolks, mustard and lemon juice together. Slowly add the oil in a steady stream, while whisking, to emulsify.

MISO MAYONNAISE

PREP TIME
— 5 minutes

MAKES
— 250 ml (9 fl oz)

— 1 egg yolk
— 1 tablespoon lemon juice
— ½ teaspoon Dijon mustard
— 1 tablespoon sweet white miso paste
— 185 ml (6 fl oz) vegetable oil

In a medium-sized bowl, whisk the egg yolk to break it up. Then whisk in the lemon juice, Dijon mustard and white miso to evenly combine. Slowly add the oil in a steady stream, while whisking, to emulsify.

SUSHI RICE

Rice is said to be the single most important element in sushi, and you must take the time to ensure that this process is done well and accurately. Sushi rice is finished in a hangiri, a wooden bowl that imparts the aroma of the wood and absorbs steam and moisture.

The vinegar flavour profile can be adjusted according to the seasons. Sushi rice in the summer and warmer months should have a slightly higher vinegar content and flavour, while in winter and cooler months you should favour a slightly sweeter seasoning.

COOK TIME
— 20 minutes + 40 minutes soaking and resting time

MAKES
— 1 kg (2 lb 4 oz/4 cups)

— 200 ml (7 fl oz) rice vinegar
— 120 g (4¼ oz) caster sugar
— 20 g (¾ oz) sea salt
— 1 x 10 cm (4 in) square kombu
— 700 g (1 lb 9 oz) short-grain sushi rice
— 900 ml (30 fl oz) cold water

Combine the vinegar, caster sugar, sea salt and kombu in a small saucepan. Heat to dissolve the sugar, then allow to cool, ready to season your hot rice.

Washing the rice is a critical part of this process. You must not be rough with your rice, or you'll break up the grains. Under gently running water, use your hands to rub the grains together until the water runs clear and all of the starch has been washed off.

Soak the rice in a large bowl of water for about 20 minutes. This will vary depending on the rice, so you want to check that each grain is two-thirds translucent.

Once soaked, you need to drain and dry the rice for 10 minutes to allow the cells to close again on the rice grains.

Place the rice in a medium-sized saucepan with a large surface area. Add the cold water. Bring to the boil and then turn the heat down to low and cook the rice for a further 8 minutes. Finally turn the heat to high for 10 seconds to lightly toast the base layer of rice. Allow the rice to sit for a further 10 minutes to plump up.

Transfer the hot rice to your wooden hangiri and use a wooden spoon to spread the hot rice around the hangiri with a swiping action. The hangiri will assist in absorbing some of the heat and steam from the rice.

Pour half of the vinegar mixture over the rice and continue using a diagonal slicing action to disperse it through the rice. Repeat with the remaining vinegar mixture. Cover with a damp cloth, ready for use.

PICKLED RED ONIONS

This pickled red onion dish has been with me for years. You can vary the flavour by using malt vinegar. Make a bigger batch and keep it in the fridge.

COOK TIME
— 30 minutes

MAKES
— 1 jar

— 400 ml (14 fl oz) sushi vinegar
— 50 g (1¾ oz) brown sugar
— 1 green chilli, sliced
— 1 star anise
— 4 red onions, sliced into rings

Warm the sushi vinegar, brown sugar, green chilli and star anise in a saucepan over a medium heat to infuse and dissolve the sugar.

Add the sliced red onion to the hot vinegar. Allow to cool and store in a jar until needed.

These onions will keep for two weeks in the fridge.

GARLIC CHIPS

This is a great little condiment to have up your sleeve. These chips add a mild garlic flavour and crispy texture to salads, tataki and other savoury dishes.

COOK TIME
— 20 minutes

MAKES
— ½ cup

— 1 large bulb garlic
— 200 ml (7 fl oz) milk
— 200 ml (7 fl oz) rice bran oil

Start by peeling your garlic cloves. Then, with either a sharp knife or a mandoline, slice the garlic into very thin slices across the clove.

Soak the sliced garlic in the milk for about 15 minuties to draw out some of the strong garlic flavour and any bitterness.

Heat the oil to about 150°C in a medium-sized saucepan.

Drain the garlic. Sprinkle it into the hot oil and fry until golden and crispy. Strain out the sliced garlic and drain on absorbent paper.

Allow to cool and store in an airtight container until required.

They will keep for a few weeks and if they go a little soft you can re-fry them.

DASHI

I learnt to make this Japanese fish stock very early on when I was living and working in Tokyo. I have never gone back to making a traditional French-style fish stock.

This recipe will always come out beautifully clear. If you can make a good builder's tea then you will be able to make dashi, as the process is pretty much the same.

COOK TIME
— 30 minutes

MAKES
— 2 litres (70 fl oz)

— 2 litres (70 fl oz) cold filtered water
— 1 x 20cm (8 in) stick kombu
— 2 cups dried bonito flakes

Pour the filtered water into a large saucepan, add the kombu and bring to a simmer but don't boil. Once simmering, add the dried bonito flakes. Simmer for 2 minutes, then turn off the heat and allow the stock to steep. The bonito flakes will rehydrate and sink.

After 20 minutes, strain the stock through a sieve. Reserve the liquid as your dashi stock and discard the kombu and bonito flakes.

Or, you can repeat the process with another 2 litres of fresh water and reuse the kombu and bonito - this is called a second dashi.

COCKTAILS
AND SHOCHU

DRUNKARD
MOJITO

PREP TIME
— 5 minutes

MAKES
— 1

This cocktail comes from a little bar in Tokyo called The Drunkard, where they serve the herbs separate from the cocktail. We have taken inspiration from this and keep the mint separate, so you crush it with your chubby straw and get the fragrance right there.

— 1 lime, halved
— 2 teaspoons palm sugar
— 30 ml (1 fl oz) white rum
— 30 ml (1 fl oz) dark rum
— 1 cup crushed ice
— 1 bunch fresh mint leaves

In a Boston shaker, muddle the lime with a muddle stick, add the palm sugar and muddle to combine. Add the rums and half of the ice. Place a glass on the shaker and shake.

Pour into your serving glass, top with the remaining ice and garnish with mint leaves.

PLUMBERRY
SOUR

PREP TIME
— 5 minutes

MAKES
— 1

This signature cocktail has been on the menu since opening. When I have friends and guests in, it is one I always recommend and a real crowd-pleaser.

— squeeze of lime juice
— squeeze of lemon juice
— 30 ml (1 fl oz) umeshu (plum wine)
— 20 ml (½ fl oz) spiced umeshu (plum wine)
— 25 ml (¾ fl oz) Damson plum vodka
— 1 teaspoon Grand Marnier
— 1½ teaspoons Chambord
— 1 egg white
— ½ teaspoon freeze-dried plum powder

Place all of the ingredients in a Boston shaker, and shake well to allow the egg white to foam.

Pour over ice and serve.

THE GOURMET

SINCE 2014

LEP

LEMON & PINEAPPLE

LwP

— 10 minutes

SERVES
— 1

This cocktail came about one night after a very busy dinner service. We were tasting some new cocktail creations and when this pineapple shochu came to the table it instantly reminded me of my childhood days when Mum and Dad would let me have L&P on the boat. It was a special treat, but this was a little different – it was L&P for adults. So we went about refining the cocktail and have since come up with our own bottle and label, giving it a new name of LwP – this is a Kiwiana cocktail.

— 90 ml (3 fl oz) pineapple shochu (see page 220)
— 15 ml (½ fl oz) spiced rum
— squeeze of lime juice
— 1 cup crushed ice
— lemonade to spritz

Add the pineapple shochu, spiced rum, lime juice and crushed ice to a cocktail shaker. Put the lid on and shake vigorously to combine the flavours and soften the ice.

Strain and serve with a spritz of lemonade.

PINEAPPLE
SHOCHU

PREP TIME
— 1 week mimimum

MAKES
— 2 litres (70 fl oz)

Pineapple shochu is one of my favourites. It is super-simple to make, and the longer you leave it the better the flavour comes out. We leave ours for up to three months to allow a really full flavour transfer. This can then be used as a base for other cocktails.

Shochu is a distilled alcoholic drink produced on Kyushu, Okinawa, and surrounding islands. At 24 per cent alcohol, it is weaker than whisky, vodka and other spirits but a little stronger than wine and sake. Shochu can be made from not only rice but also barley, sweet potato and buckwheat. We generally use rice shochu for its cleaner and balanced flavour.

— 3 good ripe pineapples
— ½ cinnamon quill
— 2 litres (70 fl oz) rice shochu

Prepare the pineapple by removing all of the skin, cutting the flesh into quarters and then removing the core.

To a large glass jar add the pineapple and cinnamon quill, pour over the rice shochu and cover with an airtight lid. Leave in a cool, dark place for at least a week to allow the flavours to infuse.

When ready to use, remove the pineapple and cinnamon, then pour the infused shochu over ice.

TAMARILLO
SHOCHU

PREP TIME
— 1 week minimum

MAKES
— 2 litres (70 fl oz)

Tamarillos were one of the fruits that I missed the most in my years overseas. So to come home and have a tree in my backyard is just brilliant. This shochu is a great way of preserving the flavour once the tamarillo season has ended. Again, with this recipe we infuse it in a chilled environment for up to three months for a full flavour extraction.

— 12 good ripe tamarillos
— 1 star anise
— 2 litres (70 fl oz) rice shochu

Prepare the tamarillos by removing all the skin and cutting them into quarters.

To a large glass jar add the tamarillos and star anise, pour over the rice shochu and cover with an airtight lid. Leave in a cool, dark place for at least a week to allow the flavours to infuse.

Remove the tamarillo and star anise, then pour the infused shochu over ice.

Eat. Drink.
Smile. Laugh.
Be. Masu.

Laughter
Joy
Prosperity

Great food,
Great wine,
Great company.
What a pleasure to be thin

Money + Happiness
+ True Love

Forever Young

家 内 安全

Be the Chang
Wish to see in
World. Om + How

でとうございます!
It's party time!
Jo

MILA
PETER
SVETLANA
DRAGAN

A Safe and
happy New Zealand
John Key
P.M.

APPROACH LOVE
WITH RECKLESS

D.L   SHARE

ACKNOWLEDGEMENTS

Where do you start when you want to thank and acknowledge the people who have helped bring your dream to life? My lifelong dream has always been to create a beautiful, contemporary Japanese restaurant and bar. This cookbook now showcases and illustrates that dream.

First of all, thanks to those closest to me – my beautiful family Kelly, Kiana and Lucas, who have travelled, eaten, listened and shared with me my passion for flavour. We have travelled the globe in search of great, unique food – fine dining and street food – in a quest to better understand our palates. Kelly is the most informed on these journeys, and is my greatest sounding-board for all things, both in restaurants and in life. Kiana, my nine-year-old, is my kitchen helper – she has been with me in the kitchen since she was four and continues to be to this day – it's awesome. Lucas is my best mate at six years old, and he is constantly testing my commitment to pure, unprocessed foods – my little legend. Without my family's passion for flavour and dedication to detail, this cookbook could not have happened.

Thank you to Mum and Dad for giving me the passion for seafood – even if it was eating raw scallops at five years old in the Hauraki Gulf!

Thanks to two great mentors and business partners – Rainer Becker and Arjun Waney. Together you taught me how to build a brand and run multiple successful operations. You are both outstanding people and the best I have met in the business!

The team at SKYCITY, Nigel Morrison, John Mortensen and Danny Bucalo, has always believed in me and given unwavering support. Together we have forged Masu into the New Zealand market and, as a result of that, we have produced this stunning book to celebrate Masu's second birthday.

Darren, Fumi, Lorraine, Liz, Meg and Brett – you are the greatest team a chef could have. You guys and gals give this restaurant soul and character. Not to mention the other 58 chefs, wait staff, bartenders, hosts, glassies and KPs who make Masu run like clockwork on a daily basis . . . Thank you!

Jenny, Leonie, and the team at Allen & Unwin, thank you for your desire to publish our story and share the myths and traditions of Japanese cuisine and create such a beautiful book.

I have to mention Babiche and Marcel together. You guys feel like my partners in crime. I had SO much fun working with you both on the endless shoot days. Babiche, your skill with the camera is sublime, and an art form I truly admire. The images are a testament to your talent. Marcel, your detail, focus and styling have given this book an exquisite look and feel. Surely we can find time for a second edition . . .

Kate, thank you for your wonderful design skills.

Alexia, thank you for making my words string together nicely and for articulating our story.

Finally, Masu would not be complete without our guests, our regulars, our friends and ultimately our extended Masu family. Keep being you and keep coming back . . .

Thank you

Nic.

INDEX

First published in 2015

Text © Nic Watt 2015

The moral rights of the author have been asserted.

Photography © Babiche Martens 2015

Allen & Unwin
Level 3, 228 Queen Street
Auckland 1010, New Zealand
Phone: (64 9) 377 3800

83 Alexander Street
Crows Nest NSW 2065, Australia
Phone: (61 2) 8425 0100
Email: info@allenandunwin.com
Web: www.allenandunwin.co.nz

A catalogue record for this book is available
from the National Library of New Zealand

ISBN 978 1 877505 58 4 NZ
ISBN 978 1 743367 65 0 UK

A catalogue record for this book is
available from the British Library.

Stylist: Marcel Gull
Design by Kate Barraclough

Printed in China by Everbest Printing Co Ltd

10 9 8 7 6 5 4 3 2 1

Australian born, Nic Watt's passion for cooking was fostered in New Zealand before honing his skills at the Park Hyatt in Tokyo, Japan. Senior positions at both the Michelin starred Nobu and the Park Hyatt in London followed before Nic made his way back to New Zealand where he headed the kitchen at the world-renowned Huka Lodge. In 2004 Nic co-founded the Roka restaurant group in London with long-time mentor and friend Rainer Becker, winning Best Oriental Restaurant at the esteemed Tio Pepe Restaurant Awards for Roka in less than a year in 2005. Global expansion followed before Nic returned to New Zealand in 2013, opening the multi-award winning Masu by Nic Watt in Auckland. He also opened Madame Hanoi in Adelaide in 2015, to excellent reviews.